This book belongs to:

_____

Gemini Daily Horoscope 2025

Author's Note: Time set to Coordinated Universal Time Zone (UT±0)

Mystic Cat
Suite 41906, 3/2237 Gold Coast HWY
Mermaid Beach, Queensland, 4218
Australia
islandauthor@hotmail.com

The information accessible from this book is for informational purposes only. No statement within is a promise of benefits. There is no guarantee of any results.

Images are under license from Shutterstock, Dreamstime, Canva, or Depositphotos.

Contents

The 12 Zodiac Star Signs

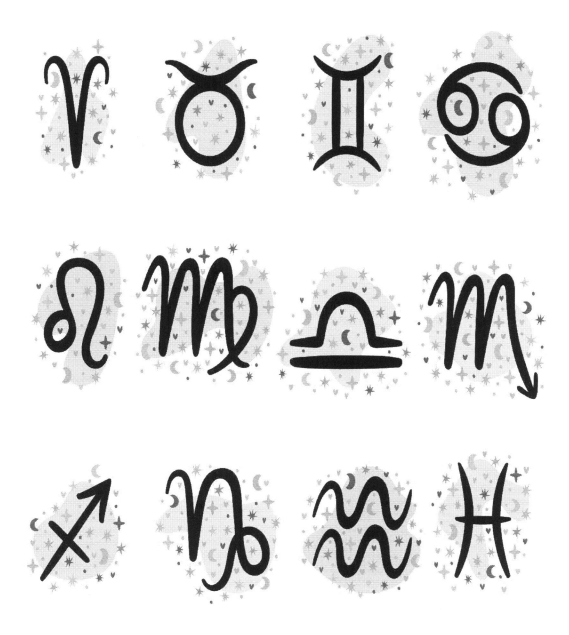

2025

January
S	M	T	W	T	F	S
			1	2	3	4
5	6	7	8	9	10	11
12	13	14	15	16	17	18
19	20	21	22	23	24	25
26	27	28	29	30	31	

February
S	M	T	W	T	F	S
						1
2	3	4	5	6	7	8
9	10	11	12	13	14	15
16	17	18	19	20	21	22
23	24	25	26	27	28	

March
S	M	T	W	T	F	S
						1
2	3	4	5	6	7	8
9	10	11	12	13	14	15
16	17	18	19	20	21	22
23	24	25	26	27	28	29
30	31					

April
S	M	T	W	T	F	S
		1	2	3	4	5
6	7	8	9	10	11	12
13	14	15	16	17	18	19
20	21	22	23	24	25	26
27	28	29	30			

May
S	M	T	W	T	F	S
				1	2	3
4	5	6	7	8	9	10
11	12	13	14	15	16	17
18	19	20	21	22	23	24
25	26	27	28	29	30	31

June
S	M	T	W	T	F	S
1	2	3	4	5	6	7
8	9	10	11	12	13	14
15	16	17	18	19	20	21
22	23	24	25	26	27	28
29	30					

July
S	M	T	W	T	F	S
		1	2	3	4	5
6	7	8	9	10	11	12
13	14	15	16	17	18	19
20	21	22	23	24	25	26
27	28	29	30	31		

August
S	M	T	W	T	F	S
					1	2
3	4	5	6	7	8	9
10	11	12	13	14	15	16
17	18	19	20	21	22	23
24	25	26	27	28	29	30
31						

September
S	M	T	W	T	F	S
	1	2	3	4	5	6
7	8	9	10	11	12	13
14	15	16	17	18	19	20
21	22	23	24	25	26	27
28	29	30				

October
S	M	T	W	T	F	S
			1	2	3	4
5	6	7	8	9	10	11
12	13	14	15	16	17	18
19	20	21	22	23	24	25
26	27	28	29	30	31	

November
S	M	T	W	T	F	S
						1
2	3	4	5	6	7	8
9	10	11	12	13	14	15
16	17	18	19	20	21	22
23	24	25	26	27	28	29
30						

December
S	M	T	W	T	F	S
	1	2	3	4	5	6
7	8	9	10	11	12	13
14	15	16	17	18	19	20
21	22	23	24	25	26	27
28	29	30	31			

2025

Daily Horoscope

GEMINI

As your astrologer, I wish to explain why one horoscope book may differ from another for each zodiac sign. The vast array of astrological activity constantly occurring in the sky requires me to focus on the essential aspect of the star sign I am writing for on any given day. Each zodiac sign is unique, and the various planetary factors affect them differently.

When crafting horoscopes, I pay special attention to the significant astrological aspects directly impacting a specific sign. By doing so, I can provide the most insightful and relevant guidance to individuals of that zodiac sign. While there might be multiple planetary alignments on a particular day, one aspect may hold more significance for a specific sign than others.

Considering the ruling planets and elements associated with each zodiac sign further refines my interpretations. This attention to detail ensures that the horoscope resonates with the distinct characteristics and tendencies of the star sign in question.

Ultimately, I aim to offer personalized insights and advice based on each zodiac sign's unique cosmic influences. By focusing on each star sign's most relevant astrological aspects, I can help readers better understand themselves and navigate the energies surrounding them. Embracing each zodiac sign's strengths, challenges, and opportunities allows me to create a horoscope book tailored to my readers' needs.

"We are born at a given moment, in a given place, and, like vintage years of wine, we have the qualities of the year and the season of which we are born. Astrology does not lay claim to anything more."

—Carl Jung

January

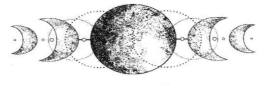

MOON MAGIC

Sun	Mon	Tue	Wed	Thu	Fri	Sat
			1	2	3	4
5	6	7	8	9	10	11
12	13	14	15	16	17	18
19	20	21	22	23	24	25
26	27	28	29	30	31	

16

NEW MOON

WOLF MOON

30 Monday

With the Moon ingress Capricorn and the arrival of the New Moon, you may feel a strong sense of determination and a desire to establish a solid foundation in various aspects of your life. You may find yourself more focused on your long-term plans. The New Moon in Capricorn encourages you to make practical decisions that align with your ambitions. It is an excellent time to prioritize your commitments, embrace structure, and progress steadily toward your objectives.

31 Tuesday

Life hums along actively and energetically, getting invitations to mingle and opportunities to head out with your broader circle of friends. A newfound endeavor ahead is a source of happiness in your life. It connects with kindred spirits who support your world. New options arrive, which bring a lovely change to your environment. It supports growth, expansion, and greater social involvement.

1 Wednesday

On New Year's Day, as the Moon enters Aquarius, you may feel a sense of excitement and anticipation for the year ahead. This lunar influence brings a fresh perspective and a desire for innovative ideas and progressive change. You might draw unconventional approaches and people as you seek to broaden your horizons and expand your circle. As you embark on this chapter, let the energy of Aquarius inspire you to break free from limitations and embrace new possibilities.

2 Thursday

Unique opportunities are incoming, which bring the magic. It offers a pivotal time for rising prospects that draw new possibilities into your life. It lets you set up growth as you spot an area for development that holds water. Working with your creativity magnifies the potential possible as you transition to a fresh start. Information arrives for you soon, which sparks your attention. Indeed, you are wise to stay open to possibilities as this adds spice and flavor to your world.

3 Friday

As Venus enters Pisces, it brings gentle and compassionate energy into your life. This cosmic alignment is a time to embrace empathy and connect deeply with your emotions and those of others. Love and creativity may take on a dreamy quality, allowing you to express yourself in imaginative and soulful ways. It's a favorable period for artistic pursuits and exploring the depths of your relationships. Allow this aspect to catalyze transformation and personal growth.

4 Saturday

As the Sun forms a sextile aspect with Saturn, it offers an opportunity to establish structure, discipline, and stability. This alignment encourages you to take practical steps towards achieving your goals and manifesting your ambitions. You may find it easier to focus on long-term objectives and make steady progress toward them. This harmonious connection between the Sun and Saturn supports your efforts to take on responsibilities, organize your life, and establish a solid foundation.

5 Sunday

With the Moon's ingress into Aries, this lunar shift ignites your passion for taking charge and initiating new beginnings. You feel a strong drive to assert your individuality and pursue your personal goals with enthusiasm, as it is a time for boldness and embracing your inner warrior spirit. Trust your instincts and embrace the courage to leave your comfort zone. As the Moon moves through Aries, you are encouraged to embrace spontaneity and independence.

6 Monday

With Mars entering Cancer, you may notice a shift in energy and motivation. Cancer's nurturing and sensitive points influence your actions, prompting you to focus more on your emotional well-being and the needs of those around you. Your assertiveness takes on a protective and nurturing tone as you strive to create a safe and harmonious environment. It's a time to pay attention to your intuition and emotional instincts, allowing them to guide your actions and decisions.

7 Tuesday

With the Moon entering Taurus, you may feel a sense of grounding and stability in your emotions. Your focus shifts towards seeking comfort, security, and sensual pleasures. You find joy in simple pleasures and indulging in activities that bring you a sense of calm and contentment. You may also experience a heightened appreciation for nature and the beauty around you. Take this opportunity to connect with your feelings and find solace in the present moment.

8 Wednesday

With Mercury entering Capricorn, you can expect a shift in your thinking and communication style. Your focus turns toward practicality, organization, and long-term planning. You become more disciplined and organized in your thoughts and conversations, seeking to express yourself with clarity and precision. Your mind shifts gears towards finding practical solutions and realistic assessments of situations.

9 Thursday

You find yourself amidst a transformative phase of personal growth that unfolds new pathways in your life. This period marks a significant leap into a fresh chapter where the horizons of your existence expand. Within this direction lies ample room for beautiful life development, offering a passage towards forthcoming options that will soon plant you in a grounded and peaceful environment. This compelling path illuminates the spotlight on your unique gifts and talents.

10 Friday

With the Moon entering Gemini, you may experience a shift in your emotional state and a heightened sense of curiosity and mental activity. Your emotions become more adaptable and changeable, reflecting the dual nature of Gemini. You may find yourself seeking variety and stimulation in your interactions and surroundings. This transit encourages you to engage in lively conversations, connect with others intellectually, and explore new ideas and perspectives.

11 Saturday

Embracing the opportunity to meet new people fosters practical connections and creates space for unique pathways that facilitate personal growth and companionship. Your efforts in nurturing a social scene bring forth invitations and networking opportunities filled with lively discussions alongside refreshing companions who add a sweet note to your life. These interactions establish grounded foundations, providing a stable basis for your world's flourishing.

12 Sunday

With the Moon entering Cancer, you may experience heightened emotional sensitivity and a stronger connection to your intuition. Your emotions become more intense and nurturing, and you seek comfort and security in familiar surroundings and close relationships. This transit encourages you to prioritize self-care and create a supportive and nurturing environment. You have a deeper understanding of your own emotional needs and the needs of others.

13 Monday

With the Sun forming a trine with Uranus and a Full Moon illuminating the sky, you enter a period of exciting and transformative energy. The Sun trine Uranus aspect brings your life a sense of liberation and individuality. You are encouraged to embrace your unique qualities and express yourself authentically. This aspect sparks creativity and originality, allowing you to break free from old patterns and embrace new, innovative ideas.

14 Tuesday

With the Moon entering Leo and Venus forming a square with Jupiter, you are entering a period filled with vibrant self-expression, amplified emotions, and expansive desires. The Moon's ingress into Leo ignites your inner spark, encouraging you to embrace your creativity. You can express your authentic self and attract attention and admiration from others. However, the square between Venus and Jupiter brings a need for balance and moderation in your desires.

15 Wednesday

Your life has witnessed many twists and turns; you've learned to navigate the highs and lows with strength and determination. This journey of growth and learning has furthered your talents, allowing you to make remarkable progress. As new options tempt you forward, you gain a unique vantage point, affording a broader overview of your path. Embracing the development of your creativity, you soon thrive in a vibrant and dynamic environment.

16 Thursday

Use the energy of the Sun to fuel your passions and drive, but also allow the influence of the Virgo Moon to plan effectively. By harnessing the precision and discernment of Virgo, you can navigate any challenges that arise from the opposing forces of the Sun and Mars. Take a measured approach and channel your assertiveness into productive and well-thought-out actions. This way, you can make the most of this dynamic energy and achieve practical outcomes.

17 Friday

With the Sun sextile Neptune, you may desire to contribute to the greater good. This aspect encourages you to trust your intuition and follow your dreams, as it brings a supportive energy that allows you to merge with Neptune's more profound, intuitive guidance. It is a time to explore your artistic and spiritual side, allowing your creativity to flow and embracing life's beauty and magic. You reveal a deeper understanding of life's beauty by aligning intentions with good deeds.

18 Saturday

This potent phase paves the way for expanding your world, with new information streaming into your life to light the pathways of rising prospects. These tidings herald a fresh beginning, ushering in a busy period filled with social engagement, networking, and invitations, fostering a supportive and connected social environment. Exploring this community setting with friends nurtures happiness, helping you groove in an environment with opportunities to mingle.

19 Sunday

As Venus conjuncts Saturn, you may feel a blend of stability and responsibility in your relationships and personal values. This aspect brings a sense of commitment and maturity, encouraging you to approach matters of the heart with seriousness and practicality. With the Sun ingress Aquarius, you embrace a more independent and forward-thinking mindset. This alignment encourages you to express your authentic self and contribute to the collective in meaningful and innovative ways.

20 Monday

The cosmos emphasizes life improvement. It mends the broken pieces and sets the stage for renewal, guiding you toward greener pastures. The ensuing expansion ushers in greater happiness, nurturing a more social environment enriched by thoughtful discussions. In the process, you facilitate companionship with someone who feels supportive, engaging, and caring, bringing an encouraging outlook that enables you to gain traction in developing your life.

21 Tuesday

As the Moon ingresses Scorpio, your emotions may become more intense and introspective. You are drawn towards deeper connections and seek emotional authenticity and depth in your relationships. The combination of the Sun conjunct Pluto and the Moon in Scorpio amplifies the transformative energy, inviting you to delve into the depths of your being and face any emotional challenges that arise. It is an opportunity for profound personal growth and empowerment.

22 Wednesday

Expanding the borders of your life enables you to move directly toward unique goals. Your inner restlessness hungers for new experiences, and the developments ahead present you with choices and decisions that align with your aspirations. You discover that settling for less is no longer necessary as you touch down in an environment ripe with blessings. Rising security and a sense of prosperity usher in good fortune to enrich your world.

23 Thursday

Mars's sextile, Uranus, infuses you with a dynamic and electric energy that fuels your drive for independence and originality. This aspect ignites your passion for taking bold actions and embracing change. You may feel a surge of excitement and a desire to break free from routine. As Mercury opposes Mars, there is a tendency for assertiveness and mental energy to clash, creating potential conflicts in communication and decision-making.

24 Friday

With the Moon ingress Sagittarius, you may feel a sense of expansion and a longing for adventure. This aspect infuses you with a desire to explore new physical and mental horizons. You may feel a renewed optimism and a craving for knowledge and experiences that broaden your understanding of the world. It is a time to embrace your adventurous spirit and seek opportunities for personal growth and discovery.

25 Saturday

With the Venus trine with Mars, a harmonious blend of passion and harmony in your relationships and desires. This aspect brings a balanced and positive energy to your interactions and pursuits of love, creativity, and personal fulfillment. Your ability to express affection is enhanced, making it easier to attract and connect with others on an intimate and romantic level. You have a magnetic charm that draws people to you, and you can navigate differences with grace and diplomacy.

26 Sunday

The Venus sextile Uranus aspect brings excitement and unexpected opportunities into your love life and social interactions. You may experience a renewed sense of freedom and liberation in your relationships and a desire for spontaneity and novelty. This alignment encourages you to embrace your unique qualities and express yourself authentically, attracting like-minded individuals who appreciate your individuality.

27 Monday

Fresh career prospects, unforeseen opportunities, and accolades that seem ordained await your embrace. The very cosmos applauds your unwavering dedication and tireless efforts, propelling you toward a stage of greater recognition and success. Once uncertain, financial matters clear like dissipating clouds after a storm. Celestial energies guide your financial decisions with wisdom and precision, allowing you to cultivate prosperity and abundance.

28 Tuesday

With Mercury ingress Aquarius, your thoughts and communication take on an innovative and progressive tone. Your mind becomes curious and open to new ideas, seeking intellectual stimulation and unconventional perspectives. You draw discussions that explore future possibilities and social issues. This placement encourages you to think outside the box and embrace your individuality in expressing yourself.

29 Wednesday

The energy of this Mercury/Pluto conjunction and the New Moon invites you to deeply introspect, examine your beliefs, and uncover any hidden motivations or fears that may hold you back. Set intentions that align with personal growth, self-empowerment, and the willingness to face and transform limiting beliefs or patterns. Embrace this conjunction's transformative energy and the New Moon's fresh energy as you embark on self-discovery and empowerment.

30 Thursday

As Uranus turns direct, innovative and revolutionary energy is unleashed. This cosmic event prompts you to embrace change and break free from stagnant patterns that may have held you back. You are encouraged to embrace your unique individuality and explore new possibilities. With the Moon's ingress into Pisces, your emotions and intuition heighten, allowing you to tap into deeper realms of creativity and spirituality.

FEBRUARY

MOON MAGIC

Sun	Mon	Tue	Wed	Thu	Fri	Sat
						1
2	3	4	5	6	7	8
9	10	11	12	13	14	15
16	17	18	19	20	21	22
23	24	25	26	27	28	

New Moon

Snow Moon

_____

_____

_____

_____

_____

_____

_____

_____

_____

_____

_____

_____

_____

_____

_____

_____

_____

_____

_____

_____

31 Friday

Exploring leads draws a beautiful result that enables you to chart a course toward achieving your goals. Streamlining and making practical changes ensures the new journey is optimized to your advantage. Please focus on the building blocks as they help you progress toward new options that resonate with your soul. This period emphasizes nurturing your home environment, laying the groundwork for a happy future.

1 Saturday

As Venus aligns with Neptune, you may find a world of beauty, love, and enchantment. This divine union brings a sense of heightened sensitivity and imagination, allowing you to experience profound emotional connections and tap into your creativity. It's a time to embrace the ethereal and the intangible, indulging in romantic ideals and appreciating the subtleties of life. You may desire harmony, compassion, and spiritual connection in your relationships.

2 Sunday

The Moon entering Aries brings dynamic energy and assertiveness. Your emotions become more spontaneous and passionate, igniting a fiery spirit within you. This lunar transit empowers you to take charge of your life and confidently pursue your desires. Allow the dynamic energy of the Aries Moon to propel you forward and inspire you to take courageous steps toward your goals. Embrace the spirit of adventure and embrace the opportunities that come your way.

3 Monday

With Mercury forming a harmonious trine with Jupiter, you reveal a heightened sense of intellect and optimism. Your mind is expansive and open to new possibilities, allowing you to think big and dream boldly. This cosmic aspect enhances your communication skills, making expressing your ideas more straightforward and engaging in meaningful conversations. Your optimism and enthusiasm are contagious, inspiring others to see the potential in their own lives.

4 Tuesday

With the Moon moving into Taurus, Venus entering Aries, and Jupiter turning direct, a decisive shift occurs in your emotional and energetic landscape. You are encouraged to embrace stability and find comfort in simple pleasures. The Taurus influence brings a sense of grounding and a focus on sensual experiences, urging you to connect with your physical surroundings and indulge in the beauty and abundance surrounding you.

5 Wednesday

News arrives, igniting the flames of optimism within your heart and expanding the horizons of your world. You're on the cusp of a transformative journey, replete with promising prospects that stir your soul. This fertile period introduces you to a dynamic and productive environment with fresh opportunities ripe for exploration. As you fan the flames of inspiration, creative energy courses through your being, providing the nourishment required to nurture your innate talents.

6 Thursday

As the Moon moves into Gemini, you reveal heightened curiosity, mental agility, and social engagement. Your mind becomes receptive, eager to explore new ideas, learn, and connect with others. This energy stimulates your communication skills, making it easier for you to express yourself and engage in meaningful conversations. Your adaptability and versatility are enhanced, allowing you to readily navigate various situations and adapt to changing circumstances.

7 Friday

Venus's sextile Pluto aspect encourages you to embrace your inner desires and explore the depths of your emotions, allowing for a profound and transformative journey of love and connection. Through this alignment, you have the opportunity to cultivate meaningful and transformative relationships that have the potential to leave a lasting impact on your life. You experience an intense emotional and romantic attraction, drawing you towards meaningful connections.

8 Saturday

With the Moon shifting into Cancer, your emotions become more tender and intuitive. You may find comfort and security in life's familiar and nurturing aspects. It is a time to prioritize self-care and create a soothing environment that supports your emotional well-being. You may feel a stronger connection to your home and loved ones, craving their presence and support. Trust your intuition as it guides you toward what brings you a sense of emotional fulfillment.

9 Sunday

Mars forming a harmonious trine with Saturn brings a blend of energy and discipline to your actions. You have the drive, motivation, and determination to pursue your goals with focused effort and strategic planning. This aspect supports you in taking decisive action and steadily progressing towards developing your ambitions. It's a good time to channel your energy into tasks that require discipline and perseverance.

10 Monday

Moon ingress Leo. You wish to be seen and appreciated for who you indeed are. This lunar influence inspires you to pursue activities that bring you joy and allow you to showcase your unique talents. Allow your inner light to shine brightly during this period, and let your creative spirit take center stage. Let your inner passion and creativity guide you as you explore new avenues for self-expression and pursue endeavors that bring you a sense of fulfillment and happiness.

11 Tuesday

Sun square Uranus. You may seek to express your individuality and rebel against any constraints hindering your growth. It's crucial to balance asserting your independence and maintaining harmonious relationships with others. Be open to innovative ideas and embrace change, as this aspect encourages you to break free from old patterns and adopt a more authentic and liberated version of yourself. Trust in your inner guidance and embrace the unique path unfolding.

12 Wednesday

During a Full Moon, the Sun and Moon are directly opposite, creating a heightened sense of illumination and emotional intensity. This phase invites you to reflect on the balance between your inner desires and outer expression. It is a time of culmination and completion, where the intentions set during the previous New Moon may come to fruition. The Full Moon brings a sense of clarity and awareness, illuminating areas of your life that may need attention or release.

13 Thursday

As the Moon enters Virgo, you may head towards a more practical and detail-oriented approach. This transit encourages you to focus on organization, productivity, and taking care of the smaller tasks that contribute to a sense of order in your life. It's an excellent time to analyze and refine your routines, paying attention to the finer details that can significantly impact your overall efficiency and well-being.

14 Friday

As Mercury moves into Pisces, you may find yourself attuned to matters of the heart and the realm of emotions. Your communication style may become gentler, more compassionate, and more intuitive, allowing you to connect more deeply with others. You can express your feelings with sensitivity and understanding, fostering empathy and creating meaningful connections. Your words carry an element of dreaminess and poetic charm, evoking emotions and touching hearts.

15 Saturday

Moon ingress Libra. Your desire for fairness and justice may strengthen, leading you to advocate for equality and harmony in your personal and social spheres. Use this time to cultivate harmonious relationships, embrace diplomacy, and find a sense of inner equilibrium. Allow the soothing energy of Libra to guide you in creating a more peaceful and graceful environment in both your inner and outer worlds.

16 Sunday

A heightened sense of your surroundings promotes expansion in your life, connecting you with unique friends who encourage you to chase your dreams. This transformative period releases stress and creates space for exciting possibilities. It's an ideal moment to channel your energy into the growth of your social life, as group activities on the horizon bring forth news and excitement, opening new doors to progress and achievement.

February

17 Monday

Curious shifts and changes usher in an improved landscape of circumstances that invigorates. The spotlight shines on the advancement of your situation, unveiling a fascinating side journey shimmering with promise. A collaborative group environment emerges, fostering lively discussions and connections with other creative individuals who resonate with your frequency. With your keen instincts, you can identify and seize the opportunities hidden within the folds of change.

18 Tuesday

As the Moon moves into Scorpio, your emotions may deepen and intensify. This transit is a time of increased emotional sensitivity and a desire to delve beneath the surface. You may find yourself drawn to introspection and exploring the hidden realms of your psyche. This transit invites you to embrace the transformative power of vulnerability and self-discovery. Simultaneously, a dreamy and imaginative energy envelops you as the Sun enters Pisces.

19 Wednesday

With diligent care, you begin to cultivate and fine-tune your skills, successfully launching them into the spotlight of a realm well worth your time and effort. Your tenacity and unwavering curiosity guide you around the corner of discovery. By exercising due diligence and proactively seeking out new job opportunities, you propel your skills to the next level. Magic weaves through your journey, stimulating growth and empowering you to manifest a gratifying outcome.

20 Thursday

Moon ingress Sagittarius. Mercury Square Jupiter. It's essential to find a balance between your enthusiasm and practicality. Use this time to engage in open-minded discussions and gather diverse insights, but also be mindful of the need for careful analysis and attention to the finer points. By harnessing the optimistic energy of Sagittarius while staying grounded, you can make the most of this period of intellectual growth and expand your understanding of the world around you.

21 Friday

A happy influence nurtures better foundations in your life. It lets you relax, enjoy carefree moments, and engage in thoughtful dialogues. Life gains momentum as invitations stream in. With a strong emphasis on life improvement, this phase leads to dynamic options that break up stagnant patterns. You replenish your emotional tanks by sharing meaningful moments with valued companions, embarking on a journey of promise and healing that soothes your restless soul.

22 Saturday

As the Moon moves into Capricorn, you can embrace a more grounded and disciplined approach to life. Capricorn's influence encourages you to prioritize practicality, responsibility, and long-term goals. This aspect is a time to focus on building a solid foundation in your personal and professional endeavors. You may find yourself more ambitious and determined to achieve success. Use this energy to establish clear plans and take deliberate steps toward your objectives.

23 Sunday

You find yourself amid a profound period of transformation that reverberates through your spirit. Your journey unfolds one step at a time, gradually constructing grounded foundations through perseverance. This phase provides a precious opportunity to reinvent as you embark on a new path towards greener pastures. Exploring possibilities empowers you to take a significant step towards expanding your world, infusing it with the richness of fresh opportunities.

24 Monday

As Mars turns direct, a surge of dynamic energy propels you forward. After a period of introspection and reflection during its retrograde phase, Mars now empowers you to take decisive action and push through any obstacles. You regain a sense of momentum and feel a strong desire to pursue your goals with vigor. This planetary shift sparks a fire within you, urging you to assert your needs, express your passions, and progress in areas that may have felt stagnant.

25 Tuesday

As the Moon ingresses into Aquarius, you may notice a shift in your emotional landscape. Aquarius brings an air of detachment and objectivity, allowing you to view situations rationally and innovatively. This lunar transit encourages you to embrace your unique qualities and express yourself authentically, even if it means going against the grain. Meanwhile, the conjunction of Mercury and Saturn amplifies your intellectual prowess and attention to detail.

26 Wednesday

This juncture in your life represents a time of transformation, propelling you toward realizing your aspirations. Your willingness to remain open to new possibilities serves as a catalyst, pushing your dreams in a unique direction. An innovative approach breaks free from restriction, guiding you to the right prospect to complement your journey. Developing grounded foundations enhances improvements in your working life, offering a solid base to spring into the future.

27 Thursday

You may feel rising intuition and emotional sensitivity as the Moon enters Pisces. This gentle and compassionate energy allows you to connect with your inner self and tune into the subtle nuances of your emotions. You may find yourself drawn to creative pursuits, spiritual exploration, and acts of kindness and empathy. Additionally, the sextile between Mercury and Uranus brings innovation and intellectual stimulation to your thoughts and communication.

MARCH

MOON MAGIC

Sun	Mon	Tue	Wed	Thu	Fri	Sat
						1
2	3	4	5	6	7	8
9	10	11	12	13	14	15
16	17	18	19	20	21	22
23	24	25	26	27	28	29
30	31					

New Moon

WORM MOON

28 Friday

New Moon. During the New Moon phase, you embark on a fresh start and set new intentions for the upcoming lunar cycle. It is a potent time to plant seeds of manifestation and initiate positive changes in your life. The energy of the New Moon encourages you to reflect on your goals and desires and to envision the future you wish to create. It is a time of introspection and self-discovery, where you can connect with your innermost dreams and aspirations.

1 Saturday

As the Moon enters Aries, you may feel fiery energy and a strong desire for action and independence. It is a time to embrace your individuality, assert yourself, and take the lead in pursuing your goals. You might feel more spontaneous, courageous, and eager to take on new challenges. Trust your instincts and be proactive in pursuing what ignites your passion. This lunar transit encourages you to be bold, take risks, and step out of your comfort zone.

2 Sunday

The Sun square Jupiter brings a dynamic tension between expansion and limitations. It calls for a balanced approach to optimism and realistic expectations. It's essential to be mindful of overindulgence or taking on too much. Use this time to gain clarity, reevaluate your beliefs, and make adjustments that align with your highest vision. Embrace the retrograde energy as an opportunity for personal growth, inner reflection, and realigning your values with your authentic self.

MARCH

3 Monday

As Mercury ingresses Aries, your communication style becomes more assertive and direct. You may find yourself speaking your mind confidently and taking a more proactive approach to expressing your ideas and opinions. This energy brings a sense of enthusiasm and a willingness to take the lead in conversations and intellectual pursuits. Simultaneously, with the Moon's ingress into Taurus, your emotional focus shifts towards stability, comfort, and sensual pleasures.

4 Tuesday

Gaining profound insights into the path ahead, you unlock new avenues of growth, and the foundations of your life grow more stable with each passing moment. This enchanted route forward is marked by the rhythmic flow of creativity through your choices and decisions, propelling you toward the realization of your dreams. Harnessing your innate talents, you blaze an enterprising trail toward developing your most cherished aspirations.

5 Wednesday

With the Moon's ingress into Gemini, your mind becomes agile and curious, craving mental stimulation and various experiences. You're more inclined to engage in lively conversations, absorb information quickly, and seek intellectual connections. The sextile between Mercury and Pluto enhances your ability to delve deep into profound subjects. Your thoughts are penetrating, and you have a knack for finding hidden truths and understanding complex concepts.

6 Thursday

Currently, you find yourself in a state of transition, a phase that may sometimes feel unsettling. Nevertheless, the wheels of progress are in motion for your life. This period highlights a journey that encompasses growth, advancement, and progress. The essence of manifestation gently nudges your focus toward developing your vision for future growth. As you explore new leads, you embark on a journey of discovery, unearthing the goodness at your life's core.

MARCH

7 Friday

With the Moon moving into Cancer, you may seek comfort, emotional security, and a sense of belonging. Your emotions become more pronounced, and you may experience empathy toward others. This ingress is a time to nurture and care for yourself and those around you. You may feel a stronger connection to your home and family, finding solace in familiar surroundings. Creating a safe and nurturing space to recharge and replenish your emotional well-being is essential.

8 Saturday

With the Sun in a harmonious trine aspect to Mars, it offers a powerful surge of energy and motivation. This alignment creates a dynamic blend of confidence, vitality, and assertiveness. You feel a strong drive to take action and pursue your goals passionately. Your self-assurance heightens, and you can assert yourself effectively in various areas of your life. Trust your abilities, harness your inner strength, and enthusiastically seize the day.

9 Sunday

When the Moon enters Leo, you reveal radiant and expressive energy. Your emotions amplify, and you strongly desire to shine and be seen. This ingress is when your inner fire and creativity ignite, inspiring you to embrace self-expression and share your unique gifts with the world. Allow your passion and enthusiasm to guide you as you engage in creative pursuits and connect with others in a heartfelt and joyful way.

MARCH

10 Monday

Exciting changes unveil a promising chapter, beckoning you to embrace adventure as you set sail toward uncharted possibilities. This period aids in establishing a unique realm that craves applying your talents. By wielding your abilities to affect positive change, your life charts a course toward rising prospects. Creating a stable platform becomes paramount, ushering in heightened security as you initiate the development of new areas, ready to bear the fruits of your labor.

11 Tuesday

Mercury conjunct Venus. When Mercury and Venus align, it brings a harmonious fusion of intellect and beauty. Your communication style becomes more charming and persuasive, allowing you to express your thoughts and ideas gracefully and eloquently. This alignment enhances your ability to connect with others on an intellectual and emotional level, making it easier to form meaningful connections and cultivate harmonious relationships.

12 Wednesday

As the Moon enters Virgo, you are encouraged to focus on practicality, organization, and attention to detail. This lunar energy brings a sense of efficiency and a desire to improve your daily routines. You may feel more inclined to analyze and evaluate your responsibilities, seeking ways to streamline your tasks and enhance productivity. With the Sun conjunct Saturn, disciplined energy is at play, urging you to take a structured approach to your goals and commitments.

13 Thursday

Embarking on a journey of exploration leads you to a treasure trove of potential just waiting to be uncovered. Your innate ability to seek out unique pathways is a remarkable gift that can significantly enhance your circumstances. As you embrace newfound possibilities and craft new goals, you open the door to a quest for learning, self-development, and personal growth. This awakening gently propels you onto an incredible journey, beckoning you toward a fulfilling life.

14 Friday

During the Full Moon, with the Sun forming a sextile with Uranus and the Moon entering Libra, you reveal a harmonizing cosmic influence. The Full Moon signifies a culmination and a time of heightened emotions and awareness. It illuminates areas of your life that may require balance and harmony. The Sun's sextile with Uranus brings excitement and novelty, encouraging you to embrace change and individuality.

15 Saturday

When Mercury turns retrograde, it signals a time of introspection and reflection for you. This celestial event invites you to slow down and reconsider your thoughts, communications, and plans. It's a period that encourages you to review and reevaluate various aspects of your life. While there may be some potential challenges and miscommunications during this time, it also presents an opportunity to gain deeper insights and clarity.

16 Sunday

Invitations to circulate with friends draw lightness and momentum into your social life. Connecting with peers brings rejuvenation and renewal into your surroundings. This period emphasizes improving home and family life, offering opportunities for companionship while engaging in innovative discussions that provide new possibilities for collaboration. Ultimately, it culminates in a happy time that offers rising prospects for your life.

17 Monday

When the Moon ingresses Scorpio, you may experience a deepening of emotions and a heightened sense of intensity. It's a time to delve into your inner world and explore the depths of your feelings. You might find yourself more introspective and inclined to introspection. This transit is an opportunity to uncover hidden truths and confront any emotional obstacles that may arise. Allow yourself to embrace the transformative energy of Scorpio and engage in self-reflection.

18 Tuesday

Harnessing your creative talents provides a solid foundation, grounding you in an environment that resonates with your unique abilities. As you initiate this distinct chapter, you leverage your skills to embark on an enterprising journey that promises momentum. With an eye on expanding your life's potential, you embark on a path that fosters growth and happiness, embracing a vibrant and fulfilling way of living.

19 Wednesday

As the Moon enters Sagittarius, it brings a sense of adventure and optimism to your emotional landscape. You may feel a strong desire to explore new horizons, both physically and intellectually. It is a time to broaden your perspectives and seek higher truths that resonate with your soul. The conjunction of the Sun and Neptune adds a touch of dreaminess and spiritual energy. You may find yourself drawn to creative pursuits or spiritual practices.

20 Thursday

The Sun enters Aries and marks the Vernal Equinox; a fresh wave of energy surges through, infusing you with the spirit of renewal and new beginnings. It is a time of awakening and stepping into your power. The Vernal Equinox signifies the arrival of spring, a season of growth and blossoming. It invites you to embrace individuality, assert yourself, and pursue your passions enthusiastically and confidently. As the days grow longer, you feel renewed vitality and purpose.

21 Friday

Venus sextile Pluto. Use this energy to dive fearlessly into your desires, knowing that the transformative power of Pluto is there to guide you toward authentic and fulfilling connections. Allow yourself to experience the beauty of deep emotional connections and their transformative power. This aspect encourages you to honor your desires and explore the profound relationships forged when you open yourself up to the transformative energy of love.

22 Saturday

Moon ingress Capricorn. Your emotions may be more reserved and focused on long-term objectives rather than immediate gratification. This lunar transit encourages you to take charge of your life and work diligently towards your aspirations. It is a good time for planning, organizing, and setting solid foundations for your future endeavors. Embrace the disciplined energy of Capricorn and use it to make progress in your personal and professional pursuits.

23 Sunday

When the Sun conjuncts Venus, a beautiful alignment occurs, bringing a harmonious blend of love, creativity, and self-expression into your life. This divine union encourages you to embrace and share your inner radiance with the world. This alignment also brings an opportunity for personal growth and transformation as the Sun sextiles Pluto, empowering you to tap into your inner strength and assert your desires.

24 Monday

Moon ingress Aquarius. Sun conjunct Mercury. This energy encourages you to embrace your uniqueness and think outside the box as you navigate social interactions and express yourself confidently and clearly. It is a time to embrace open-mindedness, new perspectives, and meaningful discussions that expand horizons and foster connections with like-minded individuals. It's an opportunity to contribute to the collective intellectual landscape.

25 Tuesday

When Mercury sextiles Pluto, you are presented with a powerful opportunity to delve into the depths of your mind and uncover profound insights. This aspect enhances your ability to research, analyze, and penetrate the core of complex subjects. You have the potential to unravel hidden information, discover hidden truths, and gain a deeper understanding of the world. This aspect also strengthens your communication skills, allowing you to convey your ideas with conviction.

26 Wednesday

When the Moon enters Pisces, you may feel a heightened empathy and compassion. Your emotions become more fluid and intuitive, allowing you to connect deeply with the feelings of others. It is a time to embrace your inner dreamer and engage in activities that nourish your soul. You may find solace in creative endeavors, such as writing, painting, or listening to music. Bring attention to your dreams and inner visions as they give you valuable insights and messages.

27 Thursday

As the Black Moon enters Scorpio and Venus moves into Pisces, you may find yourself delving into the depths of your emotions and exploring the mysteries of love and desire. The energy is intense and transformative, urging you to confront hidden desires or unresolved issues within your relationships. With Venus conjunct with Neptune, the boundaries between fantasy and reality may blur, and you can draw enchanting and dreamlike experiences.

28 Friday

Moon ingress Aries. Trust your instincts and embrace the forward momentum of this lunar transit. You are infused with vitality and confidence, inspiring you to pursue your passions and assert your individuality. Use this fiery energy to ignite your passions and embark on new beginnings. Embrace the spirit of Aries and fearlessly pursue your dreams. Allow the Moon in Aries to inspire you to be authentic, assertive, and unafraid to pursue your desires.

29 Saturday

The New Moon is an opportunity to let go of what no longer serves you and plant the seeds of your aspirations. Embrace the energy of the New Moon as a catalyst for change and transformation, and allow it to guide you toward self-discovery and personal evolution. Embrace this time of introspection and connect with your inner wisdom. Trust in the power of intention and align your actions with your deepest desires; this is a time of new possibilities and infinite potential.

30 Sunday

As Mercury moves into Pisces and joins forces with Neptune, the realm of imagination and intuition becomes amplified within you. Your mind becomes attuned to subtle energies and spiritual insights, allowing you to tap into a deeper level of understanding and connection with the unseen realms. With Neptune also transitioning into Aries, a sense of creative inspiration and individuality awakens. Your dreams and visions infuse you with newfound courage and pioneering spirit.

APRIL

MOON MAGIC

Sun	Mon	Tue	Wed	Thu	Fri	Sat
		1	2	3	4	5
6	7	8	9	10	11	12
13	14	15	16	17	18	19
20	21	22	23	24	25	26
27	28	29	30			

New Moon

_____

_____

_____

_____

_____

_____

_____

_____

_____

_____

_____

_____

_____

_____

_____

_____

_____

_____

_____

PINK MOON

31 Monday

Navigating uncharted paths grants you a distinct advantage, helping you uncover hidden gems that can elevate your career prospects. Your unwavering commitment to this journey allows you to achieve great strides while preparing meticulously for the upcoming changes. As you step into a role of added responsibility and better prospects, your persistent efforts yield a pleasing outcome, paving the way for an enriched career path.

1 Tuesday

Moon ingress Gemini. Embrace this lunar phase's playful and inquisitive nature as you embark on a journey of exploration and discovery, both within yourself and in your interactions with others. Use this time to expand your knowledge, connect with like-minded individuals, and express yourself with clarity and charm. Allow the Moon in Gemini to awaken your intellectual curiosity and inspire you to embrace the world of ideas surrounding you.

2 Wednesday

Your willingness to embrace life's challenges opens doors to unique opportunities that push the boundaries of your personal growth and development. As you work diligently to cultivate your talents, you usher in stabilizing and supportive energy, improving the day-to-day aspects of your life. Progressing toward a brighter future, you unearth an endeavor that captures your heart and time. It introduces a transformative journey, reshaping your life.

3 Thursday

As the Moon moves into Cancer, you may find yourself drawn to matters of the heart and the comforts of home. Emotions take center stage, and you become more attuned to your feelings and the needs of those around you. This lunar transit encourages you to prioritize self-care and nurturing activities. You may strongly desire emotional security and a deep connection with loved ones. It's a time to create a warm, inviting space to retreat and recharge.

4 Friday

Saturn sextile Uranus. Mars sextile Uranus. Your actions and decisions infuse with confidence as you harness the energy of Uranus, the planet of revolution and breakthroughs. Embrace this harmonious alignment as an invitation to step outside your comfort zone, take calculated risks, and manifest positive changes. Trust in your ability to adapt and transform, and let the dynamic interplay between Saturn and Uranus guide you toward a stable and exciting future.

5 Saturday

With Mars forming a harmonious trine with Saturn, you reveal a powerful blend of energy and discipline. This celestial alignment empowers you to take decisive action while incorporating careful planning and strategic thinking. You possess the drive and determination to pursue goals with great focus and perseverance. The Mars trine Saturn aspect supports you in building a solid foundation for success, allowing you to channel your ambition into productive endeavors.

6 Sunday

With the Moon moving into Leo, you brim with confidence and self-expression. Your emotions will likely be fiery and passionate, urging you to shine and embrace your authentic self. The Sun forming a harmonious sextile with Jupiter further enhances this energy, expanding your optimism and bringing opportunities for growth and abundance into your life. You may feel a surge of enthusiasm and a belief in your abilities to achieve great things.

7 Monday

With Venus conjunct Saturn, you may experience a blending of love and responsibility in your relationships and personal values. This alignment brings a sense of seriousness, commitment, and practicality to your interactions. You may seek stability, loyalty, and long-term security in your connections. This aspect encourages you to take a mature and responsible approach to matters of the heart, focusing on building solid foundations and enduring partnerships.

8 Tuesday

With Venus in sextile to Uranus, you experience a harmonious blend of love, beauty, and excitement in your relationships and personal expression. This aspect brings a touch of unpredictability and an element of surprise to your interactions, allowing for unique and stimulating connections. You draw unconventional and progressive ideas, seeking freedom and individuality within partnerships. The Moon's ingress into Virgo adds a practical tone to emotions and daily routines.

9 Wednesday

Promising signs on the horizon bolster your confidence despite some changes that may require adjustments. As you navigate these new conditions and possibilities, careful thought and planning will be your allies in shaping a positive and constructive outcome. Your rising prospects inspire heightened creativity, enabling you to deepen your knowledge and advance your skills while contributing to a brighter and more fulfilling life.

10 Thursday

As you confront life's challenges, you fortify your inner strength and resilience, and your confidence soars as you enhance your abilities. The blossoming of creativity, marked by the emergence of original ideas, empowers you to prepare meticulously for a leap of faith. As you extend your reach into uncharted territory, deepening your knowledge and heightening prospects, you embrace a proactive approach that promises transformative experiences and abundant rewards.

11 Friday

The Libra Moon invites you to embrace fairness, justice, and a sense of equilibrium in all aspects of your life. It's an opportunity to cultivate harmonious connections and create an atmosphere of tranquility both within yourself and in your interactions with others. Embrace the gentle influence of the Moon in Libra as you navigate the complexities of life, finding ways to bring more balance and peace into your world.

12 Saturday

Sharing thoughts with friends proves invaluable as you work diligently to achieve your goals and nurture your well-being. The influence of your social network serves as a powerful driver, attracting communication and invitations to social gatherings. This favorable social landscape provides the ideal setting for you to carve out a brighter path for your life. Basking in the company of friends and family becomes a harmonious and joyous note in your life's symphony.

13 Sunday

With the arrival of the Full Moon, you can embrace the illumination and culmination of energies in your life. This potent lunar phase marks a time of heightened emotions and insights, encouraging you to reflect on your deepest desires and passions. As Venus turns direct, you may experience a shift in your relationships and matters of the heart. It's a time to reassess your values, reconnect with your desires, and seek clarity in cases of love and harmony.

14 Monday

A promising pathway unfolds, bringing exciting opportunities knocking at your door. It ushers in an exhilarating phase that enables you to evolve and elevate your vision to the next level. This journey delves into areas that deepen your skills and knowledge, challenging you to seize extraordinary possibilities for growth and advancement. Here, you discover an endeavor worth your time, uncovering a golden nugget worthy of development.

15 Tuesday

Expanding your perception of what's possible uncovers leads that beckon advancement. The more you nurture your creativity and refine your abilities, the more you engage in the exciting pursuit of personal and professional growth. These positive results fuel your inspiration and drive you toward unique goals, positioning you for substantial advancement as you develop your skills. This journey enriches on multiple levels and represents a significant turning point.

16 Wednesday

Mercury's ingress into Aries adds fiery and assertive energy. You may feel more direct and confident in expressing your thoughts and ideas. This combination of the Moon in Sagittarius and Mercury in Aries encourages you to speak your truth, embrace spontaneity, and pursue your passions with renewed vigor. It's a time to trust your intuition and embrace the joy of living life to the fullest. Allow Sagittarius's adventurous spirit and Aries's boldness to guide self-discovery.

17 Thursday

Mercury conjunct Neptune immerses your mind in a sea of imagination and intuition. Your thoughts and ideas take on a dreamy and imaginative quality as you find yourself drawn to the mystical and ethereal realms. This aspect enhances your creative abilities and encourages you to explore the depths of your imagination. You may find it easier to tap into your intuition and receive insights from a higher realm of consciousness.

18 Friday

As Mars enters the fiery sign of Leo, your energy infuses with passion and courage. You feel a sense of confidence and determination, ready to take on challenges and pursue goals enthusiastically. This Mars in Leo transit ignites your creative spark and encourages you to express yourself boldly and authentically. You may find yourself drawn to activities that allow you to shine and make a statement, whether it's through your work, hobbies, or personal relationships.

19 Saturday

As the Sun gracefully moves into Taurus, you experience a grounded and sensual energy that encourages you to connect with the pleasures of life. Your focus is cultivating stability, security, and a deeper appreciation for the material world. With Mars forming a harmonious trine with Neptune, your actions are intuitive and compassionate. You find a beautiful balance between assertiveness and sensitivity, allowing you to pursue your dreams gently yet determinedly.

20 Sunday

With the Moon's ingress into Aquarius, you embrace your independent spirit and value the importance of community. You may find fulfillment in contributing to a cause or joining like-minded individuals in pursuing shared ideals. Embrace the energy of this day, celebrating the spirit of rebirth and the power of authentic connections and transformative knowledge. The harmonious influences of Venus sextile Uranus, Mercury sextile Pluto, and the Moon in Aquarius bring joy.

21 Monday

Harnessing the fiery energy of Mars with the illuminating power of the Sun, you can channel your determination and passion into constructive pursuits. This square aspect catalyzes growth and self-discovery, pushing you to cultivate resilience, assertiveness, and strategic decision-making. By embracing the lessons and opportunities that arise, you can overcome obstacles and emerge more substantial on your path toward self-realization and success.

22 Tuesday

By contemplating future possibilities and setting intentions, you'll bring your dreams into focus, boosting your confidence as you chase your vision and set lofty goals. Opportunities will arise, offering progression and advancement and propelling you into a journey of growth and refinement. Working harmoniously with your abilities, you'll channel your skills effectively and create productive change.

23 Wednesday

As the Moon gracefully moves into the ethereal realm of Pisces, you may experience sensitivity and an inclination towards introspection. Pisces's subtle and dreamy energy invites you to delve into the depths of your emotions and explore the realms of imagination. However, the challenging aspect of the Sun square Pluto adds intensity to the mix. This cosmic alignment might stir up deep-seated emotions and bring forth hidden elements of your psyche.

24 Thursday

Deep contemplation about future possibilities will crystallize your dreams into focus. Setting intentions will boost your confidence in pursuing your vision and ambitious goals. Opportunities will emerge, offering avenues for progression and advancement. This journey will promote growth and refinement, allowing you to channel your skills effectively and bring about productive change. Being open to new possibilities will help you thrive even in uncertain times.

25 Friday

As Venus aligns with Saturn in conjunction, it brings a sense of seriousness and responsibility to matters of the heart. You may desire stability and commitment in your relationships, seeking deeper connections and enduring bonds. This conjunction encourages you to evaluate your partnerships' practical aspects and establish firm foundations built on trust and loyalty. At the same time, the Moon's ingress into Aries adds fiery and assertive energy to your emotions.

26 Saturday

Upcoming opportunities are ripe with potential for development. Sharing thoughts with friends motivates, instilling the courage and drive to formulate new life plans. As creativity and concentration rise to the occasion, you gain the clarity and organization needed to pave a promising path forward. These big sky dreams present new possibilities, positioning you to expand your world outwardly and allowing you to collaborate and immerse yourself in a vibrant group environment.

27 Sunday

As Mars opposes Pluto, intense and transformative energies may arise within you. This aspect can bring power struggles, conflicts, or a need to confront deep-seated fears and desires. You might feel compelled to assert your will or challenge authority, but exercising caution and finding healthy outlets for this potent energy is essential. With the Moon entering Taurus and the arrival of a New Moon, there is an opportunity for grounding and stability amidst this intensity.

MAY

MOON MAGIC

Sun	Mon	Tue	Wed	Thu	Fri	Sat
				1	2	3
4	5	6	7	8	9	10
11	12	13	14	15	16	17
18	19	20	21	22	23	24
25	26	27	28	29	30	31

NEW MOON

FLOWER MOON

28 Monday

Embracing new opportunities sets the stage for a journey that allows your unique talents to shine brilliantly. As you extend your reach into a promising area worthy of your time and attention, focusing on working with your innate skills yields a gratifying result. This approach not only restores stability in what may have been an uncertain period but also empowers you to understand and utilize your inherent strengths for further advancement.

29 Tuesday

As the Moon enters Gemini, you crave curiosity and intellectual stimulation. This transit encourages you to engage with the world around you, connect with others, and explore new ideas and perspectives. Gemini's influence fuels your desire for social interaction and mental agility. It's a time to communicate your thoughts and ideas, engage in stimulating conversations, and seek learning and intellectual growth opportunities.

30 Wednesday

As Venus enters Aries, you may feel a surge of passion and assertiveness in matters of the heart and relationships. This fiery and independent energy inspires you to take the lead, be more spontaneous, and enthusiastically pursue your desires. You may draw new experiences and challenges, seeking excitement and adventure in your connections with others. Aries brings bold and courageous energy, encouraging you to express your authentic self and assert your needs and desires.

1 Thursday

As the Moon ingresses into Cancer, you may experience heightened emotional sensitivity and nurturance. Cancer is a nurturing and caring sign, and during this time, you may find yourself drawn to creating a warm and supportive environment for yourself and others. Your emotions may become more prominent, and you may feel a deeper connection to your inner world. It's a time to listen to your intuition and honor your emotional needs.

MAY

2 Friday

When Venus aligns with Neptune in conjunction, you may experience a heightened sense of romance, creativity, and sensitivity. This divine union invites you to explore the depths of your imagination and connect with the mystical and ethereal realms. It's a time when love and beauty intertwine, inspiring you to express your affections enchantingly. Your artistic sensibilities may heighten, allowing you to create and appreciate the beauty of art in all its forms.

3 Saturday

When the Moon enters Leo, you may feel a surge of confidence and self-expression. This fiery lunar placement encourages you to shine brightly and embrace your individuality. You are likely to exude a magnetic presence and attract attention. It is an opportune time to let your creative spirit soar and express yourself authentically. Your emotions may feel more dramatic and passionate during this lunar phase, and you might seek validation and recognition.

4 Sunday

As Pluto turns retrograde, you dive into transformation and introspection. This planetary shift invites you to explore the hidden aspects of your psyche and confront the patterns and attachments that no longer serve your growth. You are encouraged to embark on an inner journey of self-discovery and release any limiting beliefs or emotional baggage holding you back. This retrograde period offers an opportunity for profound personal evolution and rebirth.

5 Monday

When Mercury forms a harmonious sextile with Jupiter, you can expect a boost in mental clarity, communication, and expansive thinking. This aspect encourages a comprehensive perspective, seeking knowledge, and engaging in intellectual pursuits. Your mind is sharp and receptive, making it an excellent time for learning, studying, and sharing ideas. You crave philosophical discussions, seek higher truths, or explore subjects that expand your understanding of the world.

6 Tuesday

When Venus forms a sextile aspect with Pluto, you may experience a deepening of your emotional connections and an intensified passion. This harmonious alignment brings forth an opportunity for transformation and growth in your relationships and personal desires. You feel a magnetic pull towards experiences and connections that profoundly impact your heart and soul. This aspect can foster a sense of empowerment, allowing you greater intimacy and authenticity.

7 Wednesday

An idea you're soon to uncover evolves into an exciting pathway forward in your life. It provides a unique opportunity to leverage your talents and design a journey that showcases your skills to a broader audience. This enrichment phase enables you to advance your skills, be grounded in the fundamentals, and build a solid platform for your rising prospects. A fresh chapter with exciting options emerges as you refine your abilities and connect with the possibilities ahead.

8 Thursday

As the Moon enters Libra, you may seek balance and harmony in your emotional experiences. This transit encourages you to prioritize peace, cooperation, and fairness in your interactions with others. You may feel more attuned to the needs and feelings of those around you, fostering a desire for harmonious relationships and a willingness to find common ground. You can engage in diplomatic discussions and resolve conflicts gracefully and tactfully.

9 Friday

A promising gate to a refreshing environment swings open, welcoming rejuvenation and renewal into your life. Beyond these doors lie countless rising prospects, inviting you to prioritize emotional wellness. This vibrant period unfolds with unique opportunities, allowing you to reconnect with friends and reevaluate your future goals. Sharing your thoughts within this supportive environment enhances your well-being and sets the stage for a brighter future.

10 Saturday

As Mercury moves into Taurus and the Moon transitions into Scorpio, you may experience a shift in your mental and emotional energy. Mercury in Taurus makes your thinking more grounded and practical, focusing on fundamental matters. Your words carry weight, and you express yourself with conviction. Meanwhile, with the Moon in Scorpio, your emotions run deep, and you may feel a more substantial need for introspection and exploring the hidden layers of your psyche.

11 Sunday

You'll receive good news, inviting you to reconnect and share thoughts. This positive aspect emphasizes the enhancement of home and family life. The time spent with kindred spirits in these gatherings fosters a social environment that breathes new life into your energy, guiding you on a journey filled with more profound meaning and well-being. A prevailing family influence opens doors to lasting bonds filled with camaraderie and shared happiness.

MAY

12 Monday

During the Full Moon, you may experience heightened emotions and a sense of culmination or completion. This lunar phase illuminates areas of your life that require transformation and release. However, with the challenging aspect of Mercury square Pluto, you might encounter intense and potentially confrontational communication dynamics. Power struggles, secrets, and hidden agendas could surface, leading to profound and probing conversations.

13 Tuesday

Moon ingress Sagittarius is a time to nurture your freedom and explore the world with a curious and adventurous spirit. Your emotions ignite with a sense of freedom and a desire for growth. Allow yourself to break free from limiting beliefs or routines and embrace the joy of exploration and learning. This transit lets you expand your mental and emotional horizons and discover new growth and personal development possibilities.

14 Wednesday

The immense potential surrounding your life is poised to liberate you from limitations. This liberating period encourages engaging with friends in freedom-driven and fun-filled activities. As you become more involved in your social life, enthusiasm is on the upswing, prompting lively conversations focusing on supportive dialogues and deepening friendships. Under this prosperous influence, you'll wholeheartedly share with others in your broader circle.

15 Thursday

Moon ingress Capricorn. You may feel a sense of determination and ambition, seeking to progress in your professional or personal endeavors. The energy of Capricorn encourages you to organize, taking a structured approach to your tasks and projects. It's a good time for planning, strategizing, and setting realistic goals for yourself. You may also feel a more vital need for stability and security, prioritizing your financial well-being and making wise decisions for the future.

16 Friday

A social aspect adds an exciting dimension to your life, spinning tales of news and opportunity. Your confidence soars as this influence takes hold, illuminating your personality in group interactions. Attending social gatherings becomes a highlight, offering thoughtful conversations, shared happiness, and a harmonious focus on overall well-being. The music flows, and you feel deeply connected with your broader circle of friends, establishing vital and enriching bonds.

17 Saturday

When the Sun aligns with Uranus in conjunction, you may experience a desire for change and innovation. This powerful energy can bring unexpected shifts and surprises into your life, pushing you out of your comfort zone and encouraging you to embrace new possibilities. You might break free from old patterns and explore uncharted territory. This alignment can spark your creativity, originality, and individuality, empowering you to express your unique self boldly.

18 Sunday

When Mercury forms a square with Mars, there is a potential for conflicts and tensions in communication and decision-making. It's essential to be mindful of your communication style during this time and avoid jumping to conclusions or engaging in unnecessary arguments. The Moon's ingress into Aquarius adds intellectual and detached energy to the mix, encouraging you to take a more objective approach in your interactions.

19 Monday

Life is ushering in a refreshing change that will help you release areas ready for transformation. This transition signals a clean sweep of potential, propelling you toward meaning and growth in life. By nurturing your abilities, you lay the foundation for a meaningful journey forward, where your investments in time and effort yield gratifying results, ticking all the right boxes as you stride towards a brighter, more promising future.

20 Tuesday

When the Sun forms a sextile aspect with Saturn, it brings a harmonious blend of self-discipline and stability. You may find yourself more focused, organized, and willing to make the necessary effort to achieve your goals. This aspect supports long-term planning and commitment, helping you establish a solid foundation for your endeavors. With the Moon entering Pisces, your emotions may become more intuitive and sensitive.

21 Wednesday

A period of abundant opportunities unfolds in your life, ushering in a bustling and productive phase that strongly emphasizes building security and strengthening social connections. Sweeping changes are on the horizon, expanding your circle of friends and presenting you with exciting invitations and kindred spirits for companionship. You're embarking on a journey tailor-made for socializing and heading out to engage with the world.

22 Thursday

When Venus forms a harmonious trine aspect with Mars, it ignites a passionate and rhythmic energy within you. Your relationships and romantic encounters will offer the elements of desire, affection, and a balanced give-and-take dynamic. This aspect enhances your ability to express your wishes and pursue what you love with confidence and assertiveness. The Sun forms a sextile with Neptune, bringing a subtle yet dreamy energy to your life.

23 Friday

Life ushers in an expansive environment, allowing your circle of friends to flourish. This increased activity within your network connects you with a broader community of people who wield the power to influence and inspire your life. Novel ideas circulate, igniting your thoughts and paving the way for a fresh approach to life. These positive changes dispel any lingering clouds, bringing forth the radiant and warm presence of the sun overhead.

24 Saturday

When the Sun forms a harmonious trine aspect with Pluto, it brings a powerful energy of transformation and empowerment into your life. This aspect allows you to tap into your inner strength and make positive changes in your life. You may experience a deep sense of self-empowerment and the determination to overcome obstacles and challenges. With the Moon entering Taurus, you may feel a grounded and practical approach to your emotions and desires.

25 Sunday

Aries is a sign known for its boldness, initiative, and assertiveness, and as Saturn enters this sign, it brings a sense of discipline and structure to your actions and goals. You might feel compelled to take charge and tackle challenges with determination and perseverance. This period encourages you to develop a strong sense of self-reliance and to be proactive in pursuing ambitions. While Saturn's presence in Aries may present some tests, it also offers growth opportunities.

26 Monday

With Mercury entering Gemini, your mind becomes sharp and agile, ready to explore new ideas and engage in stimulating conversations. Mercury's sextile with Saturn adds a touch of practicality and discipline to your thinking process, allowing you to communicate your thoughts with clarity and precision. As the Moon enters Gemini, you feel a surge of curiosity and a desire to connect with others intellectually.

27 Tuesday

With Mercury trine Pluto, your communication and thought processes infuse with depth and intensity. You possess a keen perception and the ability to uncover hidden truths. This aspect empowers you to engage in deep conversations, research, and self-reflection, leading to profound insights and personal growth. The New Moon and the harmonious alignment between Mercury and Pluto enhance your ability to manifest your desires and make meaningful changes.

28 Wednesday

As the Moon moves into the nurturing and emotional sign of Cancer, you may feel more connected to your inner world and the people you hold dear. Your focus shifts towards home, family, and emotional well-being. This lunar transit invites you to honor your emotions and create a safe and supportive environment. You may feel a heightened sense of compassion and empathy, which can deepen your relationships and strengthen your bonds with loved ones.

29 Thursday

Unexpected news acts as a catalyst for developing unique goals, propelling your life from one success to the next. This inspiring communication infuses your world with vibrancy, drawing forth a prosperous time for connecting with your wider community. Circulating with friends takes you into a busy chapter of reshaping your goals as the pace and momentum of life lead to a period of significant growth, promoting happiness.

JUNE

MOON MAGIC

Sun	Mon	Tue	Wed	Thu	Fri	Sat
1	2	3	4	5	6	7
8	9	10	11	12	13	14
15	16	17	18	19	20	21
22	23	24	25	26	27	28
29	30					

New Moon

STRAWBERRY MOON

30 Friday

When the Sun and Mercury align, it enhances your ability to express yourself with confidence and clarity. Your thoughts and communication become more aligned, making it easier to convey your ideas to others. This transit is a good time for mental clarity and decisiveness, making it an excellent opportunity to tackle tasks requiring focus and precision. As the Moon moves into Leo, your emotions infuse with a sense of creativity and passion.

31 Saturday

A new chapter is unfolding in your life, marked by beautiful symmetry that connects you with an enriching and joyful social environment. This fresh start smoothes over rough edges and sweeps away aspects irrelevant to your life, unveiling a beautiful journey that strongly emphasizes developing companionship and nurturing friendships. This chapter lets you replenish depleted emotional reserves as you engage with people who inspire and support your life.

1 Sunday

News arrives, prompting a snap decision that opens the floodgates of possibility, bringing a sense of security and balance as you establish a grounded foundation. Your journey is evolving toward greener pastures, and staying open to new options ushers in a busy period of social engagement. Making your goals a top priority places them front and center in your life, enabling you to unveil a new chapter of fresh beginnings that expands your life toward a brighter journey.

2 Monday

As the Moon enters Virgo, you may draw practicality and attention to detail. This planetary aspect is when you can focus on organization, efficiency, and self-improvement. You may desire to analyze and evaluate situations critically, seeking ways to enhance your productivity and well-being. Your attention to detail and ability to identify areas for improvement can help you make practical adjustments in various aspects of your life.

3 Tuesday

Synchronicity guides your journey, creating the ideal environment for energy to flow as you set new goals and develop a project that charts a course toward rising prospects. Your life becomes a treasure trove of excellent options as you pave new pathways, expand your abilities into new areas, connect with individuals encouraging you to expand your horizons, and forge an enterprising path that fuels your creative inspiration.

4 Wednesday

As the Moon enters Libra, you seek harmony, balance, and cooperation in your interactions. It is a time to focus on creating harmonious relationships in your personal and professional life. You may feel a stronger desire for fairness and justice, valuing diplomacy and compromise in your interactions. You are likely to have an increased sensitivity to the needs and feelings of others, which can contribute to more harmonious and cooperative exchanges.

5 Thursday

When Venus sextiles Jupiter, it brings abundance and harmony to your relationships and experiences. You may feel a sense of joy and optimism, which can attract opportunities for growth and expansion. This alignment encourages you to embrace beauty and pleasure while seeking meaningful connections and experiences that uplift your spirit. Mercury sextile Mars amplifies mental agility and assertiveness, empowering you to communicate your ideas passionately.

6 Friday

Venus ingress Taurus is a time to nurture and cultivate your self-worth and attract abundance into your life. You may find yourself drawn to activities stimulating your senses, such as art, music, or leisure time in nature. Allow yourself to indulge in the simple pleasures and take the time to savor and enjoy the present moment. With Venus in Taurus, you can create a solid foundation for love, relationships, and the things that bring you joy and fulfillment.

7 Saturday

Moon ingress Scorpio transit encourages you to explore the hidden aspects of your psyche and confront any unresolved emotional issues. You may investigate mysteries, delve into psychological insights, or engage in transformative practices. It is a period of emotional healing and regeneration where you can release old patterns and make space for new growth. Embrace the transformative power of the Scorpio Moon and connect with your innermost self on a profound level.

8 Sunday

When Mercury conjuncts Jupiter, it expands your mind and brings a sense of intellectual growth and optimism. Ideas flow freely, and your ability to communicate and express yourself heightens. You may find yourself thinking big and envisioning new possibilities for your future. It encourages you to broaden your horizons and seek knowledge in various areas. With Mercury ingress Cancer, your thoughts and communication focus more on emotions, family, and home.

9 Monday

When Mercury squares Saturn, you may feel a sense of mental tension and restriction. It could be a time of challenges and obstacles in your communication and thinking processes. However, it also allows you to cultivate patience, discipline, and perseverance in your thoughts and words. As the Moon ingresses into Sagittarius, you may experience a shift in emotional energy, seeking adventure and new perspectives.

10 Tuesday

An exciting journey lies ahead, offering a fresh start that takes you away from difficulties and immerses you in an influx of options that enhance your abilities. Working with your skills builds stable foundations that lead to success and prosperity. This transformative journey unlocks a brighter path filled with rising possibilities for your career, rewarding you as you uncover unique options that ignite excitement and evolve into a meaningful journey forward.

11 Wednesday

During the Full Moon, you may experience heightened emotions and a sense of culmination in various areas of your life. It's a time of illumination and awareness where you can gain valuable insights and clarity. With Mercury sextile Venus, communication flows harmoniously, allowing you to express your thoughts and feelings gracefully. This cosmic aspect enhances your ability to connect with others more profoundly, fostering understanding and cooperation in relationships.

12 Thursday

When the Moon ingresses Capricorn, you may feel a shift towards more grounded and disciplined energy. This influence brings a focus on practicality, responsibility, and long-term planning. You are motivated to work diligently towards your goals, utilizing your determination and perseverance. Capricorn's influence encourages you to take charge of your life and make steady progress toward your aspirations.

13 Friday

Prioritizing your goals and developing a strategic approach allows you to focus on practical aspects that enhance your professional life. Embracing the possibilities brings a period of expansion as you stand at the crossroads, shedding outworn layers and moving toward a greener landscape of opportunity. The path ahead is clearing, ushering in improvements that advance your situation. It positions you to progress and enter a productive phase that elevates your prospects.

14 Saturday

When the Moon enters Aquarius, you may experience a shift in your emotional energy. Aquarius brings an air of innovation, independence, and intellectual curiosity to your feelings. You may find yourself seeking intellectual stimulation and engaging in thought-provoking conversations. Embrace individuality and express your unique perspective on the world. You may feel drawn to social causes and humanitarian endeavors, wanting to impact society positively.

15 Sunday

When Mars squares Uranus, there can be a sense of restlessness and an urge for change and freedom. You may seek to break free from limitations and pursue your individualistic goals. However, it's essential to be mindful of impulsive or reckless behavior during this time. On the other hand, with Jupiter square Saturn, there might be a sense of tension between expansion and restriction. You may feel pulled between taking risks and adhering to practical considerations.

16 Monday

Moon ingress Pisces. Allow yourself to embrace the fluid and intuitive nature of Pisces, and trust your inner guidance to navigate any challenges or decisions that come your way. This planetary aspect is a time for introspection, healing, and connecting with the deeper parts of your being. Find solace in solitude, engage in practices that nourish your soul, and be gentle with yourself as you journey through the waters of Pisces.

17 Tuesday

When Mars ingresses Virgo, you benefit from practical and detail-oriented energy. Virgo is an analytical and organized sign, urging you to focus on efficiency and productivity. During this time, you may be motivated to tackle tasks and projects with precision and diligence. Your attention to detail rises, and you desire to improve and refine your skills. This period encourages you to embrace a systematic approach and consider the practical aspects.

18 Wednesday

Moon ingress Aries energy can fuel your motivation and drive, inspiring you to push boundaries and overcome challenges. It's a time to trust your instincts and embrace your inner warrior. Remember to balance your assertiveness with patience and consideration for others as you navigate this dynamic phase. Trust in your ability to navigate through obstacles and embrace the fiery energy of Aries to fuel your ambitions.

19 Thursday

Jupiter's square Neptune aspect invites you to explore the boundaries of your beliefs and expand your consciousness while emphasizing the need for discernment and clear intentions. You may reassess your ideas, dreams, and long-term goals, ensuring they align with practicality and feasibility. By being mindful of the potential pitfalls of over-idealism and staying grounded in reality, you can navigate this aspect with wisdom and create a foundation for growth.

20 Friday

Life has a sweet surprise, opening up a new and exciting landscape that propels your social life forward. The kindness of others touches your heart, and a series of invitations paves the way for stable foundations in your life, welcoming new companions into your circle of friends. An array of refreshing options ushers in a jam-packed period of personal growth and world-expanding changes, ensuring your journey is anything but ordinary as you enjoy mingling with friends.

21 Saturday

When the Moon enters Taurus, and the Sun enters Cancer during the June Solstice, you may feel a sense of stability, nurturing, and emotional grounding. This alignment encourages you to create a sense of security and comfort. It's a time to connect with your emotions and prioritize self-care and nourishment. The Taurus influence brings a desire for stability, practicality, and sensual pleasures, while the Cancer energy enhances your emotional sensitivity and intuition.

22 Sunday

With Mars sextile Jupiter, you attract energy and enthusiasm to pursue goals and ambitions. This aspect ignites confidence and optimism, propelling you forward in your endeavors. You feel inspired to take on new challenges, expand your horizons, and embrace growth opportunities. Meanwhile, the Sun square Saturn introduces a touch of practicality and discipline to the mix. You may encounter obstacles that test your resolve, but this aspect demands perseverance.

23 Monday

Moon ingress Gemini. Sun square Neptune. With the Moon moving into Gemini, your mind becomes alive with curiosity and a thirst for knowledge. You find yourself seeking mental stimulation and engaging in meaningful conversations. However, the Sun's square aspect to Neptune introduces confusion and uncertainty. It can be challenging to see things clearly or make concrete decisions. You may feel a bit disoriented or disconnected from reality at times.

24 Tuesday

With the Sun aligning with Jupiter, you may experience a surge of optimism, expansion, and abundance. This powerful conjunction illuminates opportunities and invites you to reach your full potential. It's a time of personal and professional growth where you can aim high and have faith in your abilities. You are infused with confidence and enthusiasm, inspiring you to pursue your goals and dreams with unwavering determination.

25 Wednesday

With the Moon entering Cancer and the arrival of a New Moon, you are entering a potent phase of emotional renewal and new beginnings. This lunar energy invites you to turn inward, connect with your deepest emotions, and nurture yourself profoundly. The New Moon in Cancer offers a fertile ground for planting seeds of intention and setting new goals that align with your emotional well-being and personal fulfillment.

26 Thursday

With Mercury forming a sextile with Uranus and the Sun forming a sextile with Mars, there is an exciting and dynamic energy in the air. This harmonious alignment encourages you to embrace your unique ideas, express yourself confidently, and take inspired action. Mercury's ingress into Leo makes your communication style bolder and more charismatic. Your words carry a creative flair and a sense of self-assurance.

27 Friday

With the Moon moving into Leo, you reveal an exciting and dynamic phase for self-expression, confidence, and creativity. This fiery energy encourages you to shine your light and step into the spotlight with a sense of boldness and enthusiasm. It's a time to tap into your unique talents and showcase your authentic self to the world. Allow your inner passions and desires to guide you as you pursue your goals and dreams.

28 Saturday

When Mercury forms a trine aspect with Saturn, it brings a harmonious blend of practicality and intuition to your thoughts and communication. Your mind becomes focused, disciplined, and structured, allowing you to organize and plan effectively. This aspect is a favorable time for problem-solving, studying, and engaging in tasks that require attention to detail. Additionally, the trine between Mercury and Neptune enhances imagination, intuition, and creative abilities.

29 Sunday

The opposition between Mercury and Pluto brings deep-seated thoughts, emotions, and hidden truths to the surface. It's when you may uncover confidential information or encounter power struggles in your communication. Your ideas may be more probing and investigative, seeking to find the underlying motivations and dynamics. Meanwhile, the Moon's ingress into Virgo amplifies your attention to detail and desire for practicality and efficiency.

JULY

MOON MAGIC

Sun	Mon	Tue	Wed	Thu	Fri	Sat
		1	2	3	4	5
6	7	8	9	10	11	12
13	14	15	16	17	18	19
20	21	22	23	24	25	26
27	28	29	30	31		

GEMINI

NEW MOON

Buck Moon

30 Monday

You're stepping into an exciting phase of career advancement, where developing your skills paves the way for significant growth and successful outcomes. This period unlocks a treasure trove of new opportunities, attracting rising prospects and prosperity. Your endeavors position you ideally to ascend the ladder of professional success, marked by accolades that fill your world with a profound sense of achievement.

1 Tuesday

Moon ingress Libra. Use this energy to engage in meaningful conversations, practice active listening, and foster understanding in your relationships. Embrace compromise and negotiation as you navigate the various dynamics of your personal and professional life. With the Moon in Libra, you are encouraged to cultivate harmony, beauty, and grace in your interactions, creating a positive and cooperative atmosphere for yourself and those around you.

2 Wednesday

Believe that you can achieve anything you set your mind to as life becomes increasingly busy, infusing your world with energy and opportunities for outward growth. Engaging in a passion project initiates a transition into an exciting journey of growth and rising prospects, fostering your creativity and connecting you with like-minded individuals who ignite your motivation. This influx of luck generates new leads and encourages progress in your life.

3 Thursday

With renewed optimism, you step into a new chapter of your life, feeling lighter and more open to the possibilities. This vibrant phase is characterized by a lively and social environment that sparkles with potential. Life leads you into a socially connected period that supports your growth and progress and provides the perfect setting to cultivate new hobbies and connect with like-minded individuals who resonate with your approach to life.

4 Friday

As Venus enters Gemini, there is a shift towards curiosity, communication, and intellectual stimulation in matters of love and pleasure. You may be attracted to witty and versatile individuals who stimulate your mind. With Neptune turning retrograde, you are encouraged to reflect on your dreams, illusions, and spiritual connection. It's a time to reassess your ideals and dissolve any illusions hindering your growth.

5 Saturday

Breaking news breathes a gust of fresh air into your environment, revitalizing the foundations of your life and ushering in harmonious vibes. It creates a path of discovery that connects you with a more friendly landscape, providing the space for developing unique goals close to your heart. Supportive and lively discussions set the tone for a refreshing era of social involvement, as companionship and invitations bring happiness to your situation.

6 Sunday

When Venus forms sextiles with Saturn and Neptune, it brings harmonious and uplifting energy to your relationships and creative endeavors. This astrological aspect encourages you to balance practicality and imagination, allowing you to manifest your dreams with a solid foundation. You may experience a sense of stability and emotional depth in your connections with others and a heightened appreciation for beauty and artistic expression.

7 Monday

When Uranus enters Gemini, it brings intellectual curiosity and innovative thinking to your life. This transit encourages you to embrace new ideas, explore unconventional approaches, and seek academic freedom. With Venus forming a trine with Pluto, there is a powerful transformative energy in your relationships and personal values. You may experience deep emotional connections and profound shifts in your desires and attractions.

8 Tuesday

Upcoming events promise expansion in your surroundings, bringing new interests and hobbies that begin to take shape. These endeavors connect you with other creative individuals, sparking brainstorming sessions and outings. Nurturing your creativity paves the way for developing projects and goals that inspire growth, setting the stage for a productive journey in a remarkable direction. Unique projects emerge, fostering a pleasing growth cycle that expands your horizons.

9 Wednesday

With the Moon moving into Capricorn, you enter a focused determination and practicality phase. This lunar transit encourages you to prioritize your responsibilities and take a structured approach to achieving your goals. You may feel more grounded and motivated to work hard, as the Capricorn energy supports discipline and perseverance. It is a favorable time to progress in your professional life and long-term aspirations.

10 Thursday

During a Full Moon, you may experience heightened emotions and a sense of culmination. It's a time of illumination and realization, where you can gain clarity and insight into various aspects of your life. The Full Moon invites you to reflect on your accomplishments, challenges, and relationships and find balance and harmony within yourself. It's a time to release what no longer serves you and embrace the lessons and blessings that have come your way.

11 Friday

When the Moon ingresses Aquarius, you may feel a shift in your emotional landscape. Aquarius brings a sense of detachment and objectivity to your feelings, allowing you to view situations more objectively. You may be drawn to social causes and community involvement, as Aquarius is associated with collective consciousness and humanitarian ideals. This transit is a time to embrace individuality and express yourself.

12 Saturday

New options on the horizon invite you to explore a social landscape, setting the stage for opportunities to network with friends and partake in entertaining outings that enhance your well-being and happiness. A positive change is imminent, introducing a therapeutic aspect that nurtures your spirit and balances your surroundings, ultimately immersing you in a lively atmosphere filled with news and excitement.

13 Sunday

When Saturn turns retrograde, it invites you to reflect on your responsibilities, boundaries, and long-term goals. It's a period of inner evaluation and reassessment where you can review your commitments and structures. The Moon's ingress into Pisces adds a touch of sensitivity and intuition to this introspective phase. You may find yourself more attuned to your emotions and the subtle energies around you.

14 Monday

Soon, you'll find yourself settling in and appreciating the grounded foundations your hard work has laid. Your environment undergoes renewal and rejuvenation, offering a staircase of progress that propels you toward your dreams. This rejuvenated environment not only advances your skills but also nurtures your talents. You'll have the opportunity to explore a new area that holds promise for your career, fostering a sense of stability in your professional life.

15 Tuesday

Your creativity is on the rise, guiding a period of expansion in your life. This phase places you in a prime position to develop a project that introduces your work to a broader audience, allowing your talents to shine brightly. You'll connect with other creative individuals who offer their support and insight, enriching your world. Working on your vision for future growth ensures that the cream rises to the top as you progress on a path filled with inspiration and creativity.

16 Wednesday

When the Moon enters Aries, you may experience a surge of energy and assertiveness. It's a time to embrace your inner fire and take bold action toward your goals. You may feel a sense of urgency and a desire to initiate new projects or pursue personal ambitions. This fiery energy can inspire you to be more confident, courageous, and decisive in your choices. Trust your instincts and follow your passions; this is a time of self-discovery and empowerment.

17 Thursday

The more you open yourself up to new experiences and new people, the more life will offer you refreshing possibilities. If you've felt stuck in a holding pattern, breaking free from the restrictions that limit your progress is crucial. This extended period of growth allows you to create positive change in your life, widening your horizons and rewarding you with stimulating experiences that foster your growth and prosperity.

18 Friday

As Mercury forms a sextile with Venus, you have the potential for harmonious and meaningful connections with others. This aspect enhances your ability to express yourself with grace and charm, fostering positive interactions and potentially nurturing valuable relationships. Embrace the Mercury retrograde energy to reflect, realign, and adjust your communication and relationships, allowing for greater understanding and harmony.

19 Saturday

You find yourself in sync with a fortunate chapter that extends your life outwardly, opening the gate to a more social environment where you find companionship. Life hums along actively and energetically, presenting you with invitations to mingle and engage with your broader circle of friends. A newfound endeavor becomes a source of happiness, connecting you with kindred spirits who support your world.

20 Sunday

When the Moon moves into Gemini, it ignites a sense of curiosity and mental agility within you. Your mind becomes more active, and you may seek new experiences and engage in lively conversations. This transit is a time to explore different perspectives, gather information, and expand your knowledge. Your communication skills are enhanced, allowing you to express your thoughts and ideas clearly and efficiently.

21 Monday

Contemplating your future life direction introduces a new cycle of growth to consider. As you delve deeper into your future goals and aspirations, you gain insight into the path ahead, which allows you to unleash your abilities within an exciting area that tips the scales in your favor. Employing a strategic planning approach positions you in an environment that fosters outward growth, ultimately allowing you to break new ground and bask in the sunshine of new beginnings.

22 Tuesday

Moon in Cancer brings a nurturing and sensitive energy, reminding you to connect with your emotions and create a sense of emotional security within yourself and your relationships. This transit is a time to honor your feelings, nurture yourself, and seek comfort in the familiar. Meanwhile, the Sun in Leo empowers you to express your unique essence and embrace your inner strength and creativity.

23 Wednesday

With the Sun forming a sextile aspect to Uranus, you can embrace change and embrace your unique individuality. This aspect brings excitement and a desire for freedom and self-expression. It encourages you to break free from routines and explore new possibilities. Be open to unexpected opportunities and be willing to step out of your comfort zone. At the same time, Venus square Mars creates a dynamic tension between love and desire, passion and harmony.

24 Thursday

With the Sun trine Saturn, you infuse with stability, discipline, and practicality. This aspect harmonizes your goals and responsibilities, allowing you to take steady steps toward your ambitions. As the Moon ingresses Leo, your confidence and self-expression rise, encouraging you to shine your unique light and embrace your creative side. The Sun trine Neptune further enhances your imagination and intuition, opening doors to spirituality and compassion.

25 Friday

Sun opposed Pluto. Embrace the opportunity for deep introspection and inner work, allowing the transformative energy of this aspect to guide you toward a more empowered and authentic expression of yourself. Remember, you have the strength and resilience to rise above any challenges and emerge stronger on the other side. Trust in your inner power and embrace the process of transformation that unfolds before you.

26 Saturday

Moon ingress Virgo is when you can focus on refining your daily routines and seeking efficiency in your tasks. You have a heightened ability to analyze and assess situations, allowing you to make thoughtful and well-informed decisions. Your mind may be more attuned to problem-solving and practical matters as you strive for order and productivity. Use this time to tend to your responsibilities, prioritize self-care, and bring a sense of structure to your life.

27 Sunday

Something on the horizon has you reevaluating your life goals. It introduces a social environment that offers a replenishing influence. By rethinking, refining, and being open to change, you'll indulge in daydreams that creatively inspire growth. You'll enter a happy period that brings companionship and movement into your life, infusing lightness and momentum into your social life and providing heightened opportunities to mingle with friends.

28 Monday

News arrives and clears away the clouds, bringing light energy into your surroundings. A fresh possibility ignites inspiration and helps you reach for something more. Progress looms large, and creating space to nurture your dreams brings a pleasing result. Your life symbolizes fullness and richness. Working with your creativity gives you a leg up in a landscape, offering learning, growth, and possibility. Reshaping your life leads you toward growth and success.

29 Tuesday

As the Moon enters Libra, you notice a shift towards seeking harmony, balance, and fairness in your emotions and interactions. This period encourages you to build positive relationships and find common ground with those around you. You may feel a greater sense of empathy and understanding, making it easier to resolve conflicts and find compromises. Socializing and spending time with friends or loved ones can be particularly enjoyable during this time.

30 Wednesday

New options bring a creative time that promotes fun and friendship, creating a golden triangle of possibilities that improve your outlook moving forward. Remaining open to engaging with your broader circle of friends shores up any flagging foundations, taking you on a journey that offers room to grow. It provides an exciting time as improvement flow. You can use this inspiring time to turn over a new leaf in the book of your life.

31 Thursday

With Venus moving into Cancer, you might notice a shift in your emotional landscape, as this transit emphasizes nurturing and connection in your relationships. You may feel more attuned to your emotions. This period encourages you to express your feelings openly and create a safe space for others to do the same. Meanwhile, with the Moon entering Scorpio, your emotions deepen, and you may feel more inclined to explore the depths of your inner world.

AUGUST

MOON MAGIC

Sun	Mon	Tue	Wed	Thu	Fri	Sat
					1	2
3	4	5	6	7	8	9
10	11	12	13	14	15	16
17	18	19	20	21	22	23
24	25	26	27	28	29	30
31						

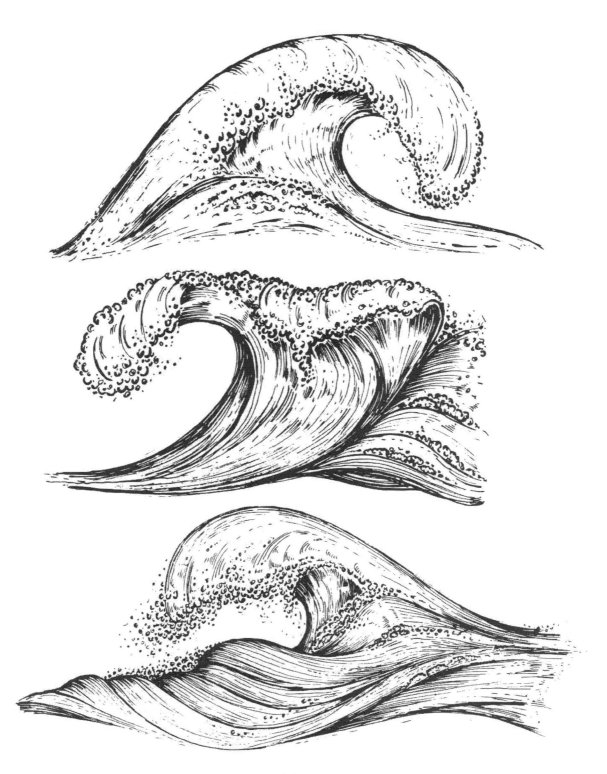

NEW MOON

STURGEON MOON

AUGUST

1 Friday

With Venus forming challenging aspects of Saturn and Neptune, you may experience tension and uncertainty in matters of love, relationships, and personal values. The square to Saturn can bring about a sense of limitation or restriction in your interactions, making it difficult to express your affection and desires fully. It may require you to confront any underlying insecurities or fears hindering your ability to form meaningful connections.

2 Saturday

The winds of change are swirling around your social life, and an openness to meeting new people draws companionship. Your enthusiasm and inspiration weave magic, aligning your energy with individuals who share your vision. This magnetic attraction fosters meaningful dialogues and positive communication that propels you forward. Upcoming opportunities to mingle encourage a phase of expansion, generating new leads and ushering in excitement and adventure.

3 Sunday

Moon ingress Sagittarius transit can bring a desire for exploration and expansion, both mentally and emotionally. You might seek new experiences and broaden your horizons through travel, learning, or connecting with people from different backgrounds. Your curiosity and enthusiasm may heighten during this time, and you might feel inspired to take risks and embrace growth opportunities. Use this time to assess your priorities, set clear intentions, and progress steadily.

4 Monday

Clear skies breeze into your life as you discover a path forward. There is a shift to a more social environment, and sharing ideas helps develop creativity. You'll embark on a journey offering heartwarming options and a supportive vibe that nurtures your spirit. This period brings an expansion time, with invitations arriving to head out and explore a community environment shared with friends. Greener pastures appear, allowing you to embark on a promising journey.

5 Tuesday

As the Moon moves into Capricorn, you may feel a shift towards a more structured and disciplined approach to your emotions and goals. This transit encourages you to take a practical and responsible stance, focusing on long-term plans and ambitions. You might find yourself drawn to tasks that require dedication and perseverance, and your emotions become grounded and stable. It's an excellent time to set realistic goals and work towards them with determination.

6 Wednesday

As Mars moves into Libra, you may seek balance and harmony in your actions and relationships. This transit encourages you to approach conflicts and challenges diplomatically and fairly. You might feel more motivated to collaborate with others and find compromises that benefit everyone involved. Use this time to focus on improving your communication skills and finding common ground with those around you.

7 Thursday

A positive trend on the horizon triggers happiness and joy, introducing a fresh opportunity to help you make tracks toward an exciting area worth your time. You'll reap the rewards of trying new endeavors as you take on a project that elevates your skills. Advancement is imminent, helping you build tangible results outward as you grow in life. It is an ideal time to explore new areas of interest. Something new offers a pathway toward success.

8 Friday

Moon ingress Aquarius. Mars trine Uranus is a favorable period for taking risks and embracing change, as you feel more confident and assertive in pursuing your goals. Embrace your individuality and use this dynamic energy to push beyond your comfort zone, seeking opportunities that align with your passions and interests. Your ability to adapt and respond to unexpected situations will be enhanced, so make the most of this adventurous and forward-thinking influence.

9 Saturday

With Mars opposing Saturn, followed by a Full Moon, and Mars opposing Neptune, you might experience various challenges and emotions. This cosmic alignment could create a sense of tension and internal conflicts. You may feel torn between asserting your desires and facing obstacles or responsibilities that seem to hold you back. The Full Moon brings heightened emotions and increased sensitivity, amplifying the impact of these oppositions.

10 Sunday

With the Moon moving into dreamy Pisces and Mars forming a harmonious trine with transformative Pluto, you may experience a powerful surge of emotions and a deep desire for growth and change. This alignment can bring a sense of emotional intensity and motivation, propelling you to take decisive actions toward your goals and ambitions. Pisces's intuitive and compassionate energy may guide you in profoundly connecting with and understanding your emotions.

11 Monday

Mercury turns direct. Miscommunications and misunderstandings that may have arisen in the past few weeks could now find resolution, and you'll likely find it easier to express yourself and understand others. It is an opportune time to move forward with plans, projects, and decisions on hold during retrograde. Embrace the forward momentum, use this period to make crucial decisions, and take action on your goals with confidence and precision.

12 Tuesday

With Saturn sextile Uranus, you will likely experience a harmonious balance between tradition and innovation. This aspect encourages creative ways to change your life while maintaining stability and structure. The conjunction of Venus and Jupiter further amplifies the positive energy, bringing opportunities for growth, abundance, and enhanced relationships. This alignment may attract opportunities for romance or financial gains.

13 Wednesday

A new journey is ready to begin in your life, emphasizing change and offering a saving grace. This new phase will enable you to double up on inspiration and work with your creativity to develop exciting dreams. A window of opportunity opens, bringing news and excitement as you touch down on a landscape ripe with blessings. It helps propel you forward toward growth and advancement. The pace of life kicks up exciting possibilities, opening a path toward development.

14 Thursday

With the Moon's ingress into Taurus, you may feel a sense of grounding and stability settling into your emotions and surroundings. Taurus is an earth sign known for its practicality and determination. During this time, you might seek comfort and pleasure in simple joys. You may feel drawn to nature, delicious food, and the company of loved ones. This period could bring a sense of contentment and a desire to build a solid foundation for your emotional well-being.

15 Friday

With Mercury sextile Mars, you may experience a surge of mental energy and sharpness. Your thoughts and communication offer assertiveness and confidence. This transit is a favorable time for problem-solving, making decisions, and acting on your ideas and plans. Your mind is quick, and you can express yourself with clarity and conviction. It's an excellent opportunity to debate, negotiate with others, or tackle intellectual challenges.

16 Saturday

With the Moon ingress Gemini, you may feel more curious and friendly. Your mind is agile, and your interests might be diverse, making it an excellent time to explore new topics or engage in stimulating conversations. Your communication skills heighten, and you may feel inclined to share your thoughts and ideas with those around you. This transit encourages you to stay open-minded and adaptable, as you might encounter various perspectives and viewpoints.

17 Sunday

Social life is about to heat up with new possibilities and invitations to enjoy time with your friends. Sharing moments with others solidifies the foundations of your life and paves the way for a happy journey forward. Sunny skies emerge, infusing your world with fun and lightness. This cultivation of interpersonal bonds launches your life towards rising prospects, empowering you to embark on an enterprising journey that inspires you to explore new horizons.

18 Monday

As Mercury forms a harmonious sextile with Mars, you may find yourself experiencing an enhanced ability to communicate with assertiveness and confidence. This cosmic alignment encourages you to express your thoughts and ideas with passion and conviction, allowing you to make a substantial impact. Meanwhile, as the Moon moves into Cancer, your emotional sensitivity deepens, creating a nurturing and caring atmosphere for yourself and others.

19 Tuesday

You're entering a time of heightened opportunity, ruling expansion as you open a pathway toward developing your dreams. Restrictions resolve as new energy flows in, bringing rejuvenation and inspiration. An area you create goes swimmingly well as you take time to build steps to achieve your vision. A rock-solid foundation provides a stable basis for growing the path. Developing abilities ignite growth, leading to rising prospects and increasing prosperity.

20 Wednesday

As the Moon enters Leo, you'll find a noticeable shift in your emotional landscape. You may experience a surge of self-expression and a desire to be seen and appreciated by others. This lunar placement encourages you to embrace creativity and confidently enter the spotlight. Your passions and enthusiasm will shine brightly, inspiring those around you. It's a beautiful time to engage in activities that bring you joy and allow your inner light to radiate.

21 Thursday

Striking the right balance in your life enhances harmony, enabling you to embrace the possibilities that lie ahead wholeheartedly. Your life becomes infused with inspiration, marking the beginning of a new chapter. Soon, you'll experience a heightened pace of lively interactions and mingling opportunities, creating an enriching phase that propels you to explore the broader potential within your social life.

22 Friday

With the Sun's entrance into Virgo, you might experience a shift in focus towards practicality and attention to detail. This period encourages you to analyze and organize aspects of your life precisely and efficiently. You'll likely feel a greater sense of responsibility and a desire to improve your skills and knowledge. This Virgo influence may also prompt you to pay more attention to your health and well-being as you seek to establish better routines and habits.

23 Saturday

As the Moon enters Virgo alongside the arrival of the New Moon, you may feel a deep sense of introspection and the opportunity for a fresh start. This lunar combination urges you to turn your attention inward, reflecting on your goals, aspirations, and areas needing improvement. It's a time for setting intentions and planting the seeds of new beginnings. Embrace the analytical energy of Virgo to assess plans meticulously, ensuring they are practical and well-organized.

24 Sunday

With the Sun forming a challenging square aspect to Uranus, you may experience a sense of restlessness and unpredictability. This cosmic alignment could bring unexpected changes and disruptions that challenge your routines and plans. You might feel a strong urge to break free from constraints and seek more independence and individuality. It's essential to be flexible and open-minded during this time, as resisting the need for change could lead to frustration.

25 Monday

With the Moon's ingress into Libra, you may seek harmony and balance in your emotions and relationships. This period encourages you to engage in cooperative and diplomatic interactions, valuing compromise and understanding. You may feel more inclined to consider the perspectives of others, fostering a sense of fairness and equality in your interactions. As Venus enters Leo, it brings a touch of extravagance and playfulness to your love life and social connections.

26 Tuesday

With Venus forming a harmonious trine to Saturn, a supportive sextile to Uranus, and another trine to Neptune, you experience emotional stability, excitement, and dreamy enchantment in personal experiences. The trine to Saturn brings commitment and reliability to your connections, allowing for steady and enduring bonds. The sextile to Uranus infuses a touch of excitement and spontaneity, encouraging you to embrace unique ways of expressing your affections.

27 Wednesday

Venus opposed the Pluto aspect, which can bring forth feelings of power struggles, jealousy, or possessiveness, potentially leading to emotional confrontations. It's essential to be aware of any hidden agendas or manipulative tendencies. While this aspect can be challenging, it offers profound growth and self-awareness. Dive deep into understanding your emotions and motivations, as this can help you navigate the complexities of your relationships with greater clarity.

28 Thursday

It's a powerful time for self-discovery, healing, and developing a greater sense of emotional resilience. Be prepared to face any emotional challenges with courage and honesty, as this can lead to profound personal growth and a deeper connection with your inner self. Embrace the transformative energy of Scorpio Moon, and allow it to guide you towards a more profound understanding of your emotions and a greater appreciation for the mysteries of life.

29 Friday

With Uranus forming a sextile aspect to Neptune, you may experience a period of enhanced creativity and spiritual insight. This harmonious alignment of the two planets can inspire you to explore new and innovative ideas, particularly in artistic or intuitive endeavors. You might find yourself drawn to unconventional approaches and alternative perspectives, seeking a deeper understanding of the interconnectedness of all things.

30 Saturday

Moon ingress Sagittarius is a favorable time to engage in activities that stimulate your mind and open your heart to different cultures and philosophies. Your curiosity heightens, and you may draw topics that broaden your worldview. Embrace the adventurous spirit of the Sagittarius Moon and use it as a catalyst to embark on external and internal journeys that can lead to profound insights and personal expansion.

31 Sunday

A time of reflection brings a complex mix of emotional awareness. Surrendering areas that have outworn their usefulness helps resolve the past, signaling that you're ready to move on. Exploring possibilities brings unique options as your path heads toward new adventures. Your creativity rises, helping you connect with a fantastic group. It brings movement and progress to your social life as you embark on a lively chapter shared with kindred spirits who brighten your life.

SEPTEMBER

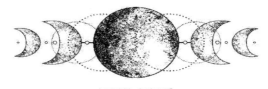

MOON MAGIC

Sun	Mon	Tue	Wed	Thu	Fri	Sat
	1	2	3	4	5	6
7	8	9	10	11	12	13
14	15	16	17	18	19	20
21	22	23	24	25	26	27
28	29	30				

New Moon

Corn/Harvest Moon

SEPTEMBER

1 Monday

Saturn ingress Pisces alignment encourages you to find structure and meaning in emotions and spirituality as you seek to harmonize your dreams and ideals with the practical aspects of life. Pisces' influence brings a sense of sensitivity and compassion to your journey. Embrace the reflective nature of this transit and use it to explore your subconscious beliefs and inner wisdom, leading to a more profound sense of self-awareness and growth.

2 Tuesday

Moon ingress Capricorn. Mercury ingress Virgo. This combination of energies supports productivity and the ability to make well-informed decisions. Embrace this period to tackle tasks with determination and clarity as you draw practical matters and a structured approach to achieving your objectives. Combining the Capricorn Moon's ambition with Mercury in Virgo's critical thinking can lay the groundwork for success and significant progress in various aspects of life.

3 Wednesday

With Mercury forming a square aspect to Uranus, you may experience a period of mental restlessness and unexpected disruptions in your thought processes. This astrological influence can change your ideas and perspectives, leading to unconventional and innovative thinking. Your mind may race with brilliant insights and flashes of inspiration, but it's essential to be cautious of impulsive decisions or reckless communication during this time.

4 Thursday

As the Moon enters Aquarius, you may experience a shift towards a more objective and open-minded emotional outlook. Aquarius' influence encourages you to detach yourself from personal biases and embrace a broader perspective on your feelings and experiences. During this lunar transit, you might feel a more substantial need for independence and individuality, valuing your uniqueness and the diversity of those around you.

5 Friday

With Mars forming a square aspect to Jupiter, you may experience energy and enthusiasm, but it's essential to be cautious of potential pitfalls during this astrological influence. Combining these planetary forces can increase ambition and confidence, motivating you to take on challenges and enthusiastically pursue your goals. However, there is a risk of overestimating your abilities and being overly optimistic, which could lead to taking on more than you can handle.

6 Saturday

As Uranus turns retrograde, you may experience a shift in the way you approach change and innovation. You might reflect on the past and reconsider previous breakthroughs and unconventional ideas during this period. This retrograde motion encourages you to assess and make changes to align with your authentic self. Simultaneously, with the Moon's ingress into Pisces, your emotions become more intuitive and sensitive, fostering greater empathy and compassion.

7 Sunday

The Full Moon marks a time of illumination and completion, as it brings to light any hidden feelings or issues that need your attention. It's a moment to reflect on your progress since the New Moon and release anything that no longer serves your highest good. This lunar phase can also bring a heightened sense of intuition and clarity, making it an ideal time for introspection and connecting with your inner wisdom.

8 Monday

As the Moon moves into Aries, you might feel a surge of energy and assertiveness. Aries' influence brings a bold and adventurous spirit to your emotions, prompting you to take charge and initiate action. During this lunar transition, you may find yourself eager to tackle challenges head-on and pursue your goals with enthusiasm. The Aries Moon encourages you to be more decisive and independent in your actions and reminds you to be mindful of impulsive reactions.

9 Tuesday

Life becomes busy as you uncover a lead worth your interest. Investing your time developing innovative goals will kickstart a trailblazing journey, helping you improve life from the ground up. You'll map out unique options, opening the path to luck and greater optimism. Essential changes will flow into your life, drawing happiness and inspiration. You'll soon make waves as you get busy developing your dreams.

10 Wednesday

The Taurus Moon fosters a sense of loyalty and perseverance, making it an excellent time to focus on long-term goals and practical matters. Embrace this steady and nurturing energy to create a harmonious environment and find inner peace amidst fluctuations. Taurus' influence brings calm and serenity, encouraging you to find comfort and security in your surroundings. Savor the present moment, relishing in the tranquil and earthy vibe of the Taurus Moon.

11 Thursday

A new assignment brings more possibilities, enabling you to assess your strengths and lean into advancement; weeding out areas that have failed to bear fruit helps you make room for more relevant projects. You'll be in your element when developing an endeavor that inspires you creatively. Being productive promotes bright optimism and outward growth. You'll create space for something unique to blossom, allowing you to establish your talents in a curious arena.

12 Friday

With the Sun forming a sextile aspect to Jupiter, you may experience a boost of optimism and a sense of expanded opportunities. This harmonious alignment can bring a favorable influence, inspiring you to take bold steps and embrace a positive outlook. As the Moon enters Gemini, you might notice a heightened curiosity and a desire to engage in lively conversations and social interactions. This lunar transit encourages you to seek mental stimulation and variety in your experiences.

13 Saturday

When the Sun is conjunct Mercury, you may experience a powerful alignment of thoughts and self-expression. This astrological aspect heightens your mental clarity and communication skills, allowing you to easily articulate your ideas and intentions. During this time, your mind is sharp and focused, making it an ideal period for making important decisions and conveying your thoughts effectively to others.

14 Sunday

Good news arrives with a flurry of excitement, marking the blossoming and growth of your social life. An invitation brightens your mood, laying the groundwork for nurturing foundations and expanding your world of possibilities. Fun and friendship become vital elements in your life, guiding you toward a more connected chapter characterized by opportunities for socializing and developing friendships.

15 Monday

Moon ingress Cancer lunar transit fosters a deeper connection to your feelings and those of others, making it a favorable time for nurturing and supporting loved ones. You may seek solace in the familiar and take a more reflective approach to your emotions. It is an excellent time to create a peaceful and cozy atmosphere at home, as the Cancer Moon encourages you to find refuge in the warmth of family and close relationships.

16 Tuesday

When Venus forms a sextile with Mars, you may experience a harmonious and balanced blend of love and passion in your relationships and personal pursuits. This astrological aspect fosters a smooth exchange of affection and attraction between you and others. Your romantic desires align with your assertive and passionate nature, making it a favorable time for initiating new connections or deepening existing ones.

17 Wednesday

Moon ingress Leo. Mercury opposed Saturn. It's essential to remain patient and avoid being overly critical of yourself or others. Embrace the Leo Moon's vibrant energy to shine brightly, and with perseverance and a thoughtful approach, you can overcome any communication hurdles posed by the Mercury-Saturn opposition. Use this time to foster confidence and self-expression while staying open to learning from others' perspectives.

18 Thursday

As Mercury moves into Libra, you may seek harmony and balance in your communication style and decision-making process. This astrological shift enhances your ability to see both sides of a situation, making you more diplomatic and fair-minded in your interactions. However, with Mercury opposing Neptune, there might be a tendency towards confusion and clouded thinking. This aspect can lead to misunderstandings or difficulties in grasping the complete picture.

19 Friday

As Mercury forms a trine to Uranus and Pluto, your mental faculties heighten, and you may experience a surge of intellectual insight and transformational thinking. This astrological combination encourages you to embrace innovative ideas and delve into profound subjects. Your thoughts and communication are potent and persuasive, making it an excellent time for expressing your ideas. With the Moon's ingress into Virgo, your emotions become more analytical and detail-oriented.

20 Saturday

When Venus forms a square aspect to Uranus, you may experience excitement and unpredictability. This astrological influence can bring unexpected events in matters of love and connection. You might crave unconventional or unique individuals, as the Uranus energy encourages novelty and independence. However, this square can also lead to conflicts or disruptions in your romantic life, as your desire for change clashes with the need for stability and commitment.

21 Sunday

Sun opposed Saturn's astrological aspect can bring a sense of heaviness and responsibility, making you feel the weight of your obligations and commitments. Staying patient and disciplined during this time is essential, as progress may seem slow, but perseverance will eventually lead to rewards. Upcoming events are poised to trigger growth in your life, paving the way for you to embark on a unique path brimming with possibilities.

22 Monday

As Mars moves into Scorpio, you may feel intense and passionate energy. This astrological event can bring a sense of determination and the desire to delve deep into your emotions and desires. With the September Equinox, you experience a significant shift in the balance of daylight and darkness, symbolizing a time of inner reflection and equilibrium. As the Sun enters Libra, you head towards finding harmony and seeking fairness in your relationships and interactions.

23 Tuesday

When the Sun is opposed to Neptune, you may experience confusion and uncertainty. This astrological aspect can bring a sense of disillusionment or a lack of clarity in your goals and self-expression. You might find it challenging to see things clearly, and your boundaries may become blurred, making it harder to discern reality from illusion. This opposition may also heighten your sensitivity and empathy, leaving you more susceptible to the emotions and energies of others.

24 Wednesday

Exploring side journeys with a sense of purpose and grace offers essential avenues for your creativity, cultivating a promising path forward. The spotlight soon shines on your unique qualities, garnering valuable feedback to help elevate your expectations for developing your skills. This exciting time propels your plans forward, enabling you to set and achieve your goals and enhance productivity. Your proactive approach leads to positive results and a pleasing outcome.

25 Thursday

New options on the horizon herald a lovely change in your environment, offering support for growth, expansion, and increased social involvement. Embracing the potential of a unique life direction helps you overcome the barriers to progress. The clear path ahead brings an open road of new adventures, enabling you to design your life with a focus on developing fresh possibilities. It fosters foundations that nurture a happy environment.

26 Friday

As the Moon moves into Sagittarius, you may experience a sense of adventure and a desire for exploration. This lunar transit encourages you to broaden your horizons and seek new experiences and knowledge. You might feel more robust optimism and enthusiasm, making it an ideal time to engage in activities that inspire and uplift you. The Sagittarius Moon also fosters a love for freedom and independence, urging you to embrace spontaneity and take leaps of faith.

27 Saturday

Your natural ability to unite people and enjoy social settings creates a lively and rewarding chapter in your life. This phase infuses your world with magic and excitement, offering opportunities for lively conversations and insightful discussions. As your emotional well-being reaches new heights, you'll feel more confident and inspired to connect with new options, promoting growth, fun, and a sense of kinship.

28 Sunday

You're on the cusp of an extended period that expands your horizons. This exciting chapter infuse your life with energy, igniting your enthusiasm and motivation. You'll focus on developing your goals, moving forward with exciting plans, and nurturing your abilities. The positive influence propels you toward greener pastures, ushering in a new source of prosperity that supports your growth. This period allows you to achieve strong personal and professional development.

OCTOBER

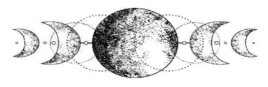

MOON MAGIC

Sun	Mon	Tue	Wed	Thu	Fri	Sat
			1	2	3	4
5	6	7	8	9	10	11
12	13	14	15	16	17	18
19	20	21	22	23	24	25
26	27	28	29	30	31	

NEW MOON

Hunters Moon

29 Monday

The Capricorn Moon enhances your ability to prioritize and organize, making it an excellent time for tackling tasks and projects that require concentration and efficiency. You may feel a stronger desire for recognition and success, which can drive you to work diligently towards your objectives. Embrace the grounded and steadfast energy of the Capricorn Moon to cultivate a sense of accomplishment and make steady progress toward your aspirations.

30 Tuesday

Your creativity is on the rise, bringing renewed inspiration into your life. You'll experience a newfound sense of freedom and expansion as you progress toward your goals. Remarkable changes on the horizon give you the green light to chase your vision for future growth. You're entering a productive and dynamic chapter that promises progress and good fortune, sweeping you along a path of advancement. You discover a promising way leading to growth and success.

1 Wednesday

As the Moon enters Aquarius, you might experience a shift towards a more open-minded and innovative perspective. This astrological influence encourages you to embrace individuality and connect with like-minded individuals. However, with Mercury square Jupiter, there may be a tendency to overextend your thoughts and ideas. It's essential to be mindful of excessive optimism and avoid making impulsive decisions based on incomplete information.

2 Thursday

Embracing new directions in your life reawakens your spirit to the vast landscape of potential that surrounds you. Soon, a side journey comes calling, tempting you forward. Exciting news is on the horizon, sparking growth, learning, and accomplishment. It marks the beginning of a beautiful time that nurtures your abilities, opens gateways to new goals, and leads you on an enterprising journey filled with exciting prospects.

3 Friday

The more you explore your talents and passions, the more doors open to advance your skills and explore new possibilities. Engaging with others who share your vision and offer support leads to social growth, harmony, and happiness. Allowing your creativity to flourish provides a breakthrough moment, infusing your life with lightness and momentum. As you dive into your creative endeavors, you'll unlock many possibilities, leaving you feeling optimistic and inspired.

4 Saturday

As the Moon moves into Pisces, you might experience heightened emotional sensitivity and a deep connection to your inner world. This astrological influence encourages you to embrace your intuition and creativity, fostering a greater understanding of your feelings and those of others. The Pisces energy allows you to tap into the subtler aspects of life, making it a favorable time for introspection, artistic expression, and spiritual pursuits.

5 Sunday

Lighter and more positive energy is coming, helping you dispel shadows and bring healing into your surroundings. This renewed energy introduces new possibilities, fostering a sense of renewal and stability. As old challenges melt away, you'll embark on a remarkable journey of personal growth. New ideas nourish and inspire while utilizing your talents opens doors to countless possibilities, leaving you hopeful—beautiful changes on the horizon signal improvement is imminent.

6 Monday

As the Moon enters Aries, you might sense a surge of vitality and a stronger desire to take charge of your emotions. This astrological influence fosters a sense of independence and assertiveness, encouraging you to be more direct in expressing your feelings. Simultaneously, Mercury's ingress into Scorpio makes your thinking more probing and intense. This combination can enhance your ability to delve into more profound subjects and uncover hidden truths.

7 Tuesday

During a Full Moon, you may experience heightened emotions and a sense of culmination in various aspects of your life. This astrological phase represents a time of heightened awareness and the illumination of what has been hidden or overlooked. It's a moment to reflect on your desires, goals, and areas where you've sought balance. However, Mercury square Pluto has the potential for intense and probing communication.

8 Wednesday

As the Moon moves into Taurus, you may experience a sense of groundedness and comfort. This astrological shift encourages you to appreciate simple pleasures and indulge in sensory delights. Taurus' energy fosters a desire for stability and connection with the physical world. At the same time, with Venus forming a sextile to Jupiter, there's a potential for joy and expansion in your relationships and pleasures.

9 Thursday

Promising prospects are on the horizon, opening new avenues in your life. Embracing adaptability and focusing on developing your skills pave the way for an enterprising chapter that leads to increased prospects. Pushing past perceived limitations reveals unique opportunities for your career. Planning and growth guide you as you navigate the development of your talents and explore new options, ultimately leading to remarkable personal and professional development.

10 Friday

Moon ingress Gemini. You might notice your mind becoming more agile and open to various viewpoints. This lunar transit also supports learning and communication, making it an ideal time to embark on intellectual pursuits or catch up on reading and learning. Embrace the Gemini Moon's energy to foster connections through engaging discussions and remain open to the endless possibilities of exploring different perspectives and embracing the joy of learning.

11 Saturday

Venus opposed Saturn's astrological aspect, which can bring feelings of distance, responsibility, or even isolation in heart matters. Awareness of any insecurities is essential, as they can influence your interactions. This opposition may prompt you to reevaluate your commitments and assess whether they align with your true desires and long-term goals. While this can be a period of increased seriousness, it's also an opportunity for growth and introspection.

12 Sunday

As the Moon moves into Cancer, you might notice a shift toward a more nurturing and emotionally sensitive state. This astrological influence encourages you to connect with your feelings deeper and seek comfort and security. Cancer's energy fosters a strong bond with family and loved ones, making it an ideal time to spend quality moments with those who matter most to you. You might find solace in familiar places and activities that evoke a sense of nostalgia.

OCTOBER

13 Monday

Libra's energy fosters a desire for fairness and cooperation, making it an excellent time to cultivate diplomacy and empathy in your relationships. You might find yourself drawn to aesthetics and the arts. This transit also encourages you to evaluate the give-and-take in your connections, seeking mutual understanding. Embrace the Venus in Libra energy to enhance social skills, foster meaningful partnerships, and infuse interactions with elegance and consideration.

14 Tuesday

Venus opposed Neptune's astrological aspect, which can bring a sense of romantic idealism, but it's essential to be cautious of unrealistic expectations. As Pluto turns direct, there's a shift in the transformative energy, encouraging you to face and embrace changes in your life. As the Moon moves into Leo, your emotions become more expressive and theatrical. Venus forming trines to Uranus and Pluto brings a harmonious blend of stability and innovation to your relationships.

15 Wednesday

A side journey may soon beckon you forward, offering unexpected opportunities for personal growth. Exciting news is also on the horizon, sparking a period of learning and accomplishment. This journey nurtures your abilities and opens new doors for development. Embracing these opportunities leads to a more extensive chapter of growth, connecting you with like-minded individuals who support your goals.

16 Thursday

As the Moon moves into Virgo, you may notice a shift towards practicality and attention to detail. This astrological influence encourages you to focus on organization and efficiency. Virgo's energy fosters a desire to analyze and improve various aspects of your routine, making it an excellent time for tasks that require precision and meticulous planning. You might feel attuned to health and well-being during this lunar transit, seeking ways to nurture your body and mind.

17 Friday

When the Sun is square to Jupiter, you may experience a period of overconfidence and the tendency to take on too much. This astrological aspect can bring a sense of optimism that might lead you to stretch your limits without considering the practicalities. While this alignment encourages growth and expansion, it's essential to be mindful of excessive risk-taking or neglecting important details. Striking a balance between enthusiasm and practicality is vital during this time.

18 Saturday

You'll crack the code to a brighter chapter, expanding your circle of friends and laying stable foundations that offer security, comfort, and growth. Riding a wave of creativity brings epiphanies, enabling you to capture unique possibilities. It allows you to rebrand your image and network with others who offer collaboration. An emphasis on improving your situation leads to a curious journey of new horizons.

19 Sunday

As the Moon moves into Libra, you may notice a shift towards a greater emphasis on harmony and relationships. This astrological transition encourages you to seek balance and cooperation in your interactions with others. Libra's energy fosters a desire for fairness and a willingness to see multiple sides of a situation. During this lunar transit, you might find yourself drawn to socializing and engaging in activities that promote connection and companionship.

20 Monday

Mercury/Mars conjunction can boost your ability to take swift and decisive action, but it's essential to be mindful of potential impulsiveness or arguments arising from a quick temper. Use this dynamic energy to tackle tasks that require focus and mental clarity while employing consideration in your interactions. Embrace the Mercury-Mars conjunction to harness your mental strength and channel it towards productive endeavors, fostering effective communication.

21 Tuesday

The New Moon astrological phase signifies setting intentions and initiating projects. As the Moon moves into Scorpio, your emotions become more intense and focused. Scorpio's energy fosters a desire to delve into deeper realms of your psyche and face any hidden truths. During this lunar transition, you might seek transformation and embrace a sense of empowerment from self-discovery. It's a time of empowerment and the potential for profound personal growth.

22 Wednesday

With Neptune moving into Pisces, you enter an astrological transition that encourages you to delve into the depths of your imagination and embrace a more intuitive and compassionate approach to life. Pisces' energy fosters a sense of connection to the unseen and the mystical, inviting you to explore your dreams and artistic pursuits and a deeper understanding of the emotional currents that flow within you.

23 Thursday

As the Sun moves into Scorpio, you may feel a shift towards more introspective and intense energy. This astrological transition encourages you to explore the deeper layers of your emotions and motivations. Scorpio's energy fosters a desire for transformation and a willingness to confront hidden truths. During this solar transit, you might crave to delve into topics often kept beneath the surface, seeking insight and understanding.

24 Friday

As the Moon moves into Sagittarius, you may feel adventurous energy and a desire for exploration. This astrological shift encourages you to embrace a more open-minded and optimistic perspective. However, with the Sun square Pluto, there may be a sense of power struggles or the need to confront deeper issues within yourself or your interactions with others. This aspect demands a balance between asserting individuality and avoiding potential control battles.

25 Saturday

With Mercury forming a trine to Saturn, you may experience a period of increased mental discipline and clarity. This astrological alignment enhances your ability to focus on tasks and communicate precisely. Your thoughts become more organized, and you might find it easier to create effective plans and strategies. This trine fosters a practical and systematic approach to problem-solving, making it an excellent time for tasks that require attention to detail.

26 Sunday

As the Moon moves into Capricorn, you may notice a shift towards a more practical and disciplined emotional state. This astrological influence encourages you to focus on your responsibilities and long-term goals. Capricorn's energy fosters a sense of determination and a willingness to work hard to achieve what you desire. During this lunar transition, you might find satisfaction in accomplishing tasks and·taking steps toward your aspirations.

27 Monday

Rising creativity leads you to circulate with friends, attending group environments with kindred spirits that bring forth a happy and relaxing time. Many hands make light work, and sharing with companions encourages collaboration, allowing room to advance. Dabbling in a creative enterprise can be therapeutic for your spirit. You'll soon team up with companions to create a creative storm, nurturing a collaboration that promotes a team effort.

28 Tuesday

Mars trine Jupiter astrological alignment enhances your drive and confidence, encouraging you to take bold actions and pursue your goals with vigor. The combination of Mars and Jupiter's energies creates a sense of expansiveness and a willingness to take calculated risks. This trine fosters a positive outlook and the potential for successful endeavors, making it an excellent time to tackle challenges and explore new opportunities.

29 Wednesday

As the Moon moves into Aquarius, you may experience a shift towards a more open and innovative emotional approach. This astrological transition encourages you to embrace your uniqueness and connect with others on a broader, more visionary level. With Mercury forming a trine to Neptune, your thoughts and communication are infused with inspiration and creativity, making it a favorable time for imaginative endeavors.

30 Thursday

With Mercury forming a sextile to Pluto, you may experience a period of intensified mental focus and transformative insights. This astrological alignment enhances your ability to delve into deep subjects and uncover hidden truths. Your thoughts become more perceptive and analytical, allowing you to understand complex matters better. This sextile encourages you to engage in meaningful conversations and research that can lead to profound discoveries.

November

MOON MAGIC

Sun	Mon	Tue	Wed	Thu	Fri	Sat
						1
2	3	4	5	6	7	8
9	10	11	12	13	14	15
16	17	18	19	20	21	22
23	24	25	26	27	28	29
30						

New Moon

BEAVER MOON

31 Friday

As the Moon moves into Pisces, you may notice a shift towards a more dreamy and intuitive emotional state. Your intuition may become more pronounced, guiding you toward a deeper understanding of your emotions and the subtleties of the world around you. Embrace the Pisces Moon's energy to nurture your soul, engage in acts of kindness, and explore the spiritual dimensions of existence as you navigate this heightened sensitivity and emotional depth.

1 Saturday

New options ahead let you dip your feet into a social landscape. It sets the stage for opportunities to network with friends. It brings entertainment and outings that draw well-being and happiness. A positive change ahead illustrates a therapeutic aspect that nurtures your spirit. It gets more balance into your surroundings, and you soon settle into enjoying a lively atmosphere. It brings news and change in a flurry of excitement.

2 Sunday

Moon ingress Aries astrological shift encourages you to take the initiative and approach your emotions enthusiastically. Aries' energy fosters a desire for action and independence. However, with Venus square Jupiter, there's potential for overindulgence and unrealistic expectations in matters of the heart. This aspect can bring forth a need to balance your desires with a realistic assessment of what's achievable.

3 Monday

You can do anything you set your mind to achieving. Life becomes busy as the pace around your world picks up steam. It brings a lively time that offers to grow your life outwardly. A passion project brings a transition to an exciting journey of growth and rising prospects. It heightens creativity and connects you with others who fire up motivation. Drawing luck into your life generates new leads that offer progression.

4 Tuesday

With Mars forming a trine to Neptune, you may experience a period of heightened creativity and inspired action. This astrological alignment empowers you to infuse your pursuits with imagination and sensitivity, allowing your actions to flow effortlessly. As Mars moves into Sagittarius, your energy becomes more adventurous and enthusiastic. This transition encourages you to take bold steps toward your goals and embrace a more expansive approach to your endeavors.

5 Wednesday

During a Full Moon, you may experience a heightened culmination of emotions and intentions. This astrological phase marks a time of realization and illumination, where your feelings and desires come to the forefront. The Full Moon's energy encourages you to take stock of your progress, achievements, and any areas needing adjustments. It's a potent time for letting go of what no longer serves you and embracing a sense of completion.

6 Thursday

Mars sextile Pluto astrological alignment empowers you to harness your inner strength and progress significantly toward your goals. As the Moon moves into Gemini, your emotions become more adaptable and communicative. It is a favorable time for engaging in conversations and learning from diverse perspectives. With Venus moving into Scorpio, your relationships and passions could take on a more intense and profound quality.

7 Friday

Good news arrives in a flurry of excitement. Things turn for the better when your social life blossoms and grows. An invitation appears, which brightens your mood. Nurturing foundations brings a wellspring of possibilities into your life. Fun and friendship light a welcoming journey toward a more connected chapter in your life. Opportunities to socialize are a source of inspiration that shines a light on developing friendships.

8 Saturday

Uranus ingress Taurus astrological transition encourages you to embrace change and adaptability in your approach to finances and the material world. However, with Venus squaring Pluto, there's potential for intense emotional experiences in relationships and matters of the heart. This aspect can bring forth power struggles and a need for transformation in how you relate to others. As the Moon moves into Cancer, your emotions may become more nurturing and sensitive.

9 Sunday

As Mercury turns retrograde, you may experience introspection and reflection. This astrological phenomenon often brings a slowing down and encourages you to review, revise, and reconsider your plans and communications. It's a time to be mindful of potential misunderstandings or technical glitches, as Mercury's apparent backward motion can sometimes create communication challenges. Use this retrograde phase to revisit projects or reconnect with people from the past.

NOVEMBER

10 Monday

With the Moon moving into Leo, you may notice a shift toward a more expressive and outgoing emotional state. This astrological transition encourages you to embrace your inner creativity and seek opportunities for self-expression. Leo's energy fosters a desire for recognition and a willingness to share talents with others. During this lunar transit, you might find yourself drawn to activities that allow you to shine and be at the center of attention.

11 Tuesday

Jupiter's retrograde is a time to revisit your plans, seek wisdom from within, and focus on inner growth rather than outward achievements. Embrace the Jupiter retrograde energy as a chance to refine your path, explore new philosophical insights, and cultivate a deeper understanding of the broader meanings in your life's journey. This period encourages you to trust in inner transformation, even if it means temporarily shifting your focus from external pursuits.

12 Wednesday

With Mercury forming a conjunction with Mars, you may experience heightened mental activity and assertiveness in your communication style. This astrological alignment empowers you to express your thoughts and ideas directly and confidently. Your mind becomes more focused and decisive, making it a favorable time for making decisions and acting on your plans. As the Moon moves into Virgo, your emotions become more analytical and detail-oriented.

13 Thursday

Expanding horizons brings a quick uptick of potential. A fresh cycle beckons for your life, and it removes the deadwood. It enables you to grow a blossoming path forward. It offers a journey that promotes renewal and rejuvenation. A strong emphasis on improving your foundations draws more security, which helps shift your focus toward developing functional areas. Rising prospects have you thinking about the possibilities.

14 Friday

Events ahead bring expansion into your surroundings. It supplies new interests, and you soon find these hobbies nicely taking shape. It connects you with other creative people who offer brainstorming sessions. Nurturing creativity brings an active time of developing projects and goals that inspire growth. It hits the ticket for a productive time to move your life in a remarkable direction. Unique projects crop up to bring a pleasing cycle of change that expands your horizons.

15 Saturday

As the Moon moves into Libra, you may notice a greater emphasis on harmony and balance in your emotions and interactions. This astrological transition encourages you to seek fairness and cooperation in your relationships. Libra's energy fosters a desire for companionship and a willingness to find common ground. During this lunar transition, you might find yourself drawn to social activities and engaging in conversations that create understanding and unity.

16 Sunday

You sync up with a lucky chapter that expands life outwardly. It opens the gate to a more social environment, bringing people into your life who offer companionship. Life hums along actively and energetically, getting invitations to mingle and opportunities to head out with your broader circle of friends. A newfound endeavor ahead is a source of happiness in your life. It connects with kindred spirits who support your world.

17 Monday

The Sun-Jupiter trine enhances your confidence and encourages you to embrace opportunities with an open heart. Simultaneously, the Sun-Saturn trine brings a sense of structure and responsibility, helping you make steady progress. The Mercury sextile Pluto aspect adds depth to your communication, encouraging meaningful conversations and insights. As the Moon moves into Scorpio, your emotions may become more intense and introspective.

18 Tuesday

Unexpected news is about to materialize, offering you an inspiring assignment. A new option helps you move towards growth with a plan in place. It brings a shift forward that offers to advance your skills and grow your abilities. It brings a venture that harnesses the essence of manifestation, allowing you to settle into a productive groove that holds fantastic appeal for your life. Imagination and creativity run wild, drawing a journey of growth and evolution.

19 Wednesday

Mercury ingress Scorpio astrological transition encourages you to delve deeper into matters, seeking hidden truths and uncovering insights beneath the surface. The Mercury-Uranus opposition can bring unexpected disruptions to your thoughts and conversations, encouraging you to be flexible and open to new perspectives. Yet, the Mercury-Neptune trine adds a touch of intuition and creativity to your communication, fostering empathy and imaginative expression.

20 Thursday

During a New Moon, you may experience a fresh start and a time of setting intentions. This astrological phase marks a period of new beginnings, inviting you to plant seeds of your desires and aspirations. With the Sun conjunct Mercury, your thoughts and communication align with your core identity, facilitating clear expression and a focused mindset. As Mercury moves into Sagittarius, your thinking becomes more expansive and open to new perspectives.

21 Friday

As the Sun forms an opposition to Uranus, you may experience changes and disruptions. This astrological aspect can bring restlessness and a desire for freedom. Be prepared for surprises and the need to adapt to shifting circumstances. However, the Sun's trine to Neptune adds a harmonious influence, allowing you to tap into your intuition and creativity. This combination encourages you to balance embracing change and staying connected to your dreams.

22 Saturday

As the Sun moves into Sagittarius, you may feel a shift towards a more adventurous and optimistic energy. This astrological transition encourages you to explore new horizons and embrace a broader perspective. With Mercury forming a trine to Saturn, your thinking becomes more disciplined and focused, allowing you to tackle tasks and communicate clearly. As the Moon moves into Capricorn, your emotions may align with a sense of determination and responsibility.

23 Sunday

With the Sun forming a sextile to Pluto, you may experience a deeper understanding of your motivations. This astrological alignment empowers you to tap into your power and make changes that align with your authentic self. This sextile encourages you to explore the depths of your psyche and embrace your potential for growth and renewal. It's a favorable time to shed light on any hidden truths and address underlying issues that may have been holding you back.

24 Monday

You soon can settle in and appreciate the grounded foundations of your hard work. Your environment goes through renewal and rejuvenation, creating stairs of progress that help you climb higher toward your dreams. It brings an environment that advances your skills and nurtures your talents. It lets you dip your feet into a new area with promise for your working life. As you transition onward, you benefit from a more stable landscape.

25 Tuesday

With Mercury forming a conjunction with Venus, you may experience a period of heightened communication and social harmony. This astrological alignment empowers you with a charming and diplomatic way of expressing your thoughts and feelings. Your interactions may become more pleasant, and your ability to convey your ideas more persuasive. As the Moon moves into Aquarius, your emotions may become more detached and innovative.

26 Wednesday

With Venus forming trines to Jupiter and Saturn, you may experience a balanced and harmonious energy in matters of love, relationships, and values. This astrological alignment empowers you with ease and stability in your interactions. The Venus trine Jupiter aspect encourages positive experiences and expansion in matters of the heart, potentially bringing new opportunities or enhancing existing connections.

27 Thursday

Pisces' energy fosters a sense of sensitivity and a desire to seek solace in creative or spiritual pursuits. During this time of gratitude and togetherness, you might find yourself more attuned to the emotions of those around you and drawn to acts of kindness and generosity. It is a moment to embrace the true spirit of Thanksgiving by nurturing your emotional well-being, connecting with loved ones, and reflecting on the abundance of love and understanding in your life.

28 Friday

As Saturn turns direct, you may feel a shift in the cosmic energy influencing your responsibilities and long-term goals. This astrological event marks a time when the planet Saturn begins to move forward in its orbit, allowing you to move forward more effectively with your plans and ambitions. Saturn, often associated with discipline and structure, turning direct can bring a sense of increased clarity and a feeling of obstacles and challenges slowly easing up.

29 Saturday

Mercury's direct astrological event marks the end of a period of potential miscommunications, delays, and technical glitches that can occur during Mercury's retrograde. With Mercury moving forward, you can expect a smoother flow in your daily interactions and a more remarkable ability to make decisions and confidently express yourself. It's a reasonable time to implement the insights and reflections you've gained during the retrograde phase.

30 Sunday

Moon ingress Aries astrological shift encourages you to take the initiative and follow your desires with determination. However, as Venus opposes Uranus, there may be unexpected twists and turns in matters of the heart or your values, which could lead to a need for greater flexibility and adaptability. Yet, the Venus trine Neptune aspect brings a touch of imagination and compassion to your relationships and desires, fostering a sense of connection and understanding.

DECEMBER

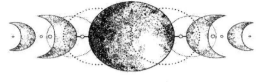

MOON MAGIC

Sun	Mon	Tue	Wed	Thu	Fri	Sat
	1	2	3	4	5	6
7	8	9	10	11	12	13
14	15	16	17	18	19	20
21	22	23	24	25	26	27
28	29	30	31			

New Moon

Cold Moon

1 Monday

Rising creativity sees that things are on the move in your life. It rules the time of increasing expansion that places you in the box seat to grow your talents. You develop a project that brings your work to a broader audience, and this sees your star shining brightly. It makes you contact other creative types who get support and connection into your world. Working on your vision for future growth brings the cream to the top.

2 Tuesday

As the Moon moves into Taurus, you may notice a shift towards a more grounded and practical emotional state. This astrological transition encourages you to seek comfort, stability, and sensory pleasures in your surroundings. Taurus' energy fosters a sense of patience and a desire for security. With Venus forming a sextile to Pluto, your relationships and passions take on a deeper, more passionate tone. Use the Venus-Pluto sextile to explore the depths of emotions and connections.

3 Wednesday

Your unique qualities shine in the spotlight soon. It garners feedback that enables you to grow your expectations around developing your skills. It offers an exciting time as your plans get shifted forward. Following through on setting your goals brings a project that increases productivity. It does enable you to kick up a storm and deepen your knowledge in an area that inspires growth in your life. It helps you achieve growth by imbuing your life with potential and possibility.

4 Thursday

Moon ingress Gemini astrological phase marks a time of culmination and illumination, where emotions and thoughts emerge. You might feel a surge of curiosity and a desire to engage in meaningful conversations or share your ideas with others. Gemini's energy fosters a sense of adaptability and a thirst for knowledge, making it an ideal time to gather information and seek clarity on matters close to your heart.

5 Friday

You enter an energizing time that gets you involved in growing your life. You dabble in new interests, which opens up a path of growth. A change of scenery ahead draws a rejuvenating influence. You open a new page on your book of life and start manifesting your dreams as you develop your life towards unique goals. Being proactive enables you to generate positive results and reach a pleasing outcome.

6 Saturday

As the Moon moves into Cancer, this astrological transition encourages you to focus on your inner world and seek comfort in familiar settings. Cancer's energy fosters a desire for emotional connection and security, making it an ideal time to spend with loved ones and create a warm and nurturing atmosphere. Additionally, with Mercury forming a trine with Neptune, your communication takes on a more intuitive and empathetic quality.

7 Sunday

The more you open your life to new people and experiences, the more life reaches you with refreshing possibilities. If you feel stuck in a tense holding pattern, being mindful of breaking free of the restrictions that limit progress in your life enables you to devise a winning approach. It brings an extended time, allowing you to create positive life changes. Your thirst for life widens your horizons and rewards you with stimulating experiences that help you grow and prosper.

8 Monday

Your working life is headed towards expansion as rising prospects bring a busy and dynamic environment. Being open to advancement helps catapult you to the next level in your career. Maintaining excellence draws growth as you receive opportunities that increase your career's potential. It does bring heightened security and a pleasing result to your working goals. A lovely perk arrives, which is a feather in your cap.

9 Tuesday

With Mars forming a square to Saturn, you might experience a sense of frustration or obstacles in your path. This astrological aspect can bring challenges to taking action and pursuing your goals. It may feel like you're trying to move forward but encountering resistance or delays. While this can be frustrating, evaluating your plans and strategies is also an opportunity. Consider whether you need to adjust or exercise patience in certain areas.

10 Wednesday

With the Moon moving into Virgo, you may experience a shift towards a more practical state. This astrological transition encourages you to pay attention to the finer points of your daily life and to seek organization and efficiency in your routines. Virgo's energy fosters a desire for order and to take care of practical matters. Additionally, with Neptune turning direct, you'll likely notice greater clarity in matters related to your dreams, intuition, and spiritual pursuits.

11 Thursday

With Mercury forming a trine to Neptune, you may experience a period of heightened intuition and imaginative thinking. This astrological alignment empowers you with creativity and spiritual insight in your communication and thought processes. As Mercury moves into Sagittarius, your review style becomes more expansive and open-minded, encouraging you to explore new ideas and embrace a broader perspective.

12 Friday

Moon ingress Libra astrological transition encourages you to seek fairness, cooperation, and beauty in your surroundings. This astrological transition encourages you to seek cooperation in your interactions with others. Libra's energy fosters a desire for companionship and a willingness to find common ground. During this lunar transit, you might draw social activities, artistic pursuits, or conversations that aim to create understanding and unity.

13 Saturday

With Mercury forming a sextile to Pluto, your communication and thought processes take on a more profound and insightful dimension. This astrological aspect encourages you to delve deep into matters, seek hidden truths, and uncover transformative insights. It's a favorable time for intense and meaningful conversations, as well as for research and investigative thinking. You'll likely have a keen sense of intuition and an ability to penetrate to the core of complex issues.

14 Sunday

When Mars forms a square aspect to Neptune, you might experience confusion, low energy, or challenges in pursuing your goals. This astrological aspect can create friction between your desires for action and Neptune's nebulous, sometimes illusory influence. It's as if your drive and motivation are clouded by uncertainty or even deception. You may find it challenging to assert yourself or take decisive action, and your energy levels may fluctuate.

15 Monday

Moon ingress Scorpio. Mars ingress Capricorn. This combination of energies prompts you to approach your goals with determination and a strategic mindset. It's a time to channel your emotional intensity into productive endeavors, allowing you to make significant progress. Embrace the Scorpio Moon's energy to engage in meaningful self-reflection, and use Mars in Capricorn's influence to work towards your aspirations with unwavering focus and resilience methodically.

16 Tuesday

News arrives, which kicks off an exciting chapter. It triggers an active phase of developing goals as you become involved with the broader world of potential around your life—a cycle of growth that blossoms into a meaningful path forward. The seeds planted become an inspiring journey for your social life. Connecting with friends brings a sense of optimism that smooths over the rough edges. A new approach takes prominence as rising confidence draws vitality.

17 Wednesday

With the Sun forming a square to Saturn, you may encounter a sense of tension and responsibility in various aspects of your life. This astrological aspect can bring obstacles and challenges that test your patience and resilience. It's as though a weight or restriction is holding you back from freely expressing yourself or pursuing your goals. However, as the Moon moves into Sagittarius, you'll feel a shift towards a more optimistic and adventurous emotional state.

18 Thursday

You crack the code to a brighter chapter for expanding your circle of friends. It helps you lay stable foundations that provide security, comfort, and growth. Riding a wave of creativity brings epiphanies that help you capture unique possibilities. It allows you to rebrand your image and network with others who offer collaboration. An emphasis on improving your situation brings a curious journey of new horizons.

DECEMBER

19 Friday

Something on offer has you re-evaluating your life goals. It brings a social environment that draws a replenishing influence. Rethinking, refining, and being open to change help you splurge on daydreams that creatively inspire growth. You enter a happy time that brings companionship. Lightness and momentum surround your social life as you head towards heightened opportunities to mingle with friends. It brings a busy transition towards new possibilities.

20 Saturday

With the arrival of the New Moon, you stand at the threshold of a new beginning. This astrological event marks a fresh lunar cycle, inviting you to set intentions and plant seeds. It's a time for introspection, reflection, and considering what you wish to manifest. As the Moon moves into Capricorn, you're encouraged to approach your goals with determination, practicality, and responsibility. Capricorn's energy supports ambitions and reminds you to build solid foundations.

21 Sunday

Sun square Neptune's astrological aspect can create a fog that blurs the boundaries between reality and illusion, making it essential to exercise caution in decision-making. Simultaneously, Venus square Saturn adds a touch of restriction and possible challenges in the heart and finances. However, with the December Solstice and the Sun's ingress into Capricorn, you'll feel a significant winter shift (or summer in the Southern Hemisphere).

22 Monday

Moon ingress Aquarius astrological transition encourages you to embrace your individuality and engage in social and intellectual pursuits that foster community and innovation. Aquarius' energy is marked by a desire for freedom and a willingness to explore unconventional ideas. You might be drawn to causes promoting change and humanitarian values during this lunar transit. Use this cosmic influence to express and connect with like-minded individuals.

23 Tuesday

You soon team up with companions to brew up a creative storm. A trailblazing aspect nurtures a collaboration that promotes a team effort. You connect with different groups of people and assemble a team that helps create fun and happiness in your social life. Your core group of people supports your energy and brings invitations to expand the borders of your world. A lively time offers unique ideas for potential development.

24 Wednesday

Venus square Neptune's astrological aspect can cast a romantic and dreamy veil over your relationships and desires, but it also carries the potential for miscommunication and misunderstandings. It's essential to exercise caution and ensure that your ideals align with the practical aspects of your life during this time. As Venus enters Capricorn, you'll feel a shift towards a more grounded and responsible approach to love and values.

25 Thursday

On Christmas Day, as the Moon moves into Pisces, you may experience a heightened sense of empathy and emotional connection with the world around you. This astrological shift encourages you to embrace the spirit of compassion and togetherness often associated with the holiday season. Pisces' energy fosters a dreamy and imaginative atmosphere, making it an ideal time for sharing stories, spreading love, and embracing the season's magic.

26 Friday

Goals swirling around your mind get a chance to launch soon. Creativity rises, and this favors circulating with friends. Attending a group environment with kindred spirits lifts the lid on a happy and relaxing time. Many hands make light work, and choosing to share with companions brings a collaboration that offers room to advance life forward. Dabbling in a creative enterprise is healing and therapeutic for your spirit.

27 Saturday

Moon ingress Aries. You might be motivated to start new projects, initiate plans, or tackle tasks you've been putting off during this time. Use this cosmic influence to channel your inner drive and determination, allowing yourself to leap into action and make the most of the opportunities that come your way. Embrace the Aries Moon's dynamic energy to assert your needs and desires, and don't be afraid to step boldly into the adventures that await you.

28 Sunday

A shift ahead brings fundamental changes to your social life. It opens your world to new companions, and this expansion offers a liberating side to life. It lights up pathways of personal growth that help you remove any restrictive boxes that may currently limit your life's potential. Clearing the path forward brings transformation and is instrumental in cracking the code to a brighter chapter. A new approach draws rejuvenation and renewal.

29 Monday

With the Moon moving into Taurus, you may notice a more grounded and stable emotional state. This astrological transition encourages you to seek comfort and security in your surroundings. Taurus' energy fosters a desire for simplicity and a connection to the physical world. You might enjoy indulging your senses through good food, soothing music, or a leisurely walk in nature. This lunar influence invites you to slow down, savor the moment, and prioritize self-care.

30 Tuesday

When Mercury squares Saturn, you may face challenges communicating and processing information. Your thoughts and ideas might encounter resistance or obstacles that make it difficult to express yourself effectively. You could feel mental pressure or self-doubt, causing you to second-guess your words and decisions. Cultivating patience and persistence is essential, as overcoming these hurdles can lead to valuable personal growth.

31 Wednesday

On New Year's Eve, when the Moon ingresses into Gemini, you may feel lightness and curiosity in the air. This astrological shift can inspire you to be friendly and intellectually engaged during your celebrations. You'll likely find yourself drawn to lively conversations, seeking out a variety of topics and mingling with a diverse group of people. Your mind is agile, making adapting to social situations easier and initiating exciting dialogues with others.

1 Thursday

You may encounter a perplexing start on New Year's Day with Mercury squaring Neptune and Mercury ingressing into Capricorn. Communication and decision-making could become foggy or unclear, as Neptune's influence tends to cast an ethereal veil over your thought processes. Your logical thinking may clash with a tendency toward daydreaming. However, you'll likely regain focus and practicality as Mercury moves into structured Capricorn.

Astrology, Tarot & Horoscope Books.

Mystic Cat

Mystic Cat Tarot

In Relationship Reading
$15.00
Crossroads
$10.00
Next Relationship Reading
$15.00

Ohoroscope@Hotmail.com

Made in United States
Orlando, FL
08 December 2024

55231460R00098